THE ART OF
LIVING
OTHER
PEOPLE'S
LIVES

THE ART OF
LIVING
OTHER
PEOPLE'S
LIVES

Stories, Confessions, and
Memorable Mistakes

GREG DYBEC

Running Press
PHILADELPHIA

Books published by Running Press are available at special discounts for
bulk purchases in the United States by corporations, institutions, and
other organizations. For more information, please contact the Special
Markets Department at Perseus Books, 2300 Chestnut Street, Suite 200,
Philadelphia, PA 19103, or call (800) 810-4145, ext. 5000, or e-mail
special.markets@perseusbooks.com.

ISBN 978-0-7624-5993-3
Library of Congress Control Number: 2016934633

E-book ISBN 978-0-7624-6107-3

10 9 8 7 6 5 4 3 2 1
Digit on the right indicates the number of this printing

Cover and interior design by Ashley Todd
Edited by Jessica Fromm
Typography: DIN Condensed and Minion Pro

Running Press Book Publishers
2300 Chestnut Street
Philadelphia, PA 19103-4371

Visit us on the web!
www.runningpress.com

To Mom and Dad,
for never considering my dreams
anything other than reality.

Contents

Introduction

I'm one of the few people who think they were born in the right decade.

I grew up in the nineties, so I can still remember a time when the Internet wasn't the Internet it is today, back when cell-phone screens were black and white. I was a wide-eyed college student majoring in English when I watched the Internet blossom into a place where inexperienced writers could share their thoughts and reach a wider audience than most established authors. I didn't dare admit it in my literature classes, where we studied the works of eighteenth-century greats, but I wanted so badly to be part of the new digital gold rush that so many unknown writers were capitalizing on. I also wanted real books like the one you're holding now; but I'm a millennial, so I never once thought I couldn't have my cake and eat it, too.

After college I spent some time working a mind-numbing retail job, interning once a week, and freelance writing for failing websites. I knew I wanted more, and finally an opportunity came along that I thought could be my big break. I took a job at Elite Daily. At the time, the website was less than two years old and had a ramshackle staff consisting of college dropouts and first-time writers. Luckily, my decision to come on board was the right choice. Shortly after I joined the team, the site exploded onto the digital-publishing scene in Justin Bieberesque fashion, quickly becoming one of the most widely read websites in the world. Through articles on dating, news, and the honest millennial experience, we began reaching millions of readers, and it was nothing short of amazing.

My secret college dreams had taken shape. I was part of the new digital wave that was taking over the Internet, and I didn't even have to wear a shirt and tie to work. The Elite Daily team was just a small group of twentysomethings with little to no professional experience who ended up turning a passion project into a globally recognized media company. It was the greatest natural high I could have hoped for. I was living the modern-day American Dream in which white picket fences were replaced with page views, and 401(k)s meant nothing in comparison to Twitter followers.

As with any good thing, there was a trade-off. After some time, I couldn't help but feel I was losing a part of my real-life identity to my Internet personality. The term IRL (in real life) is like a safe word for millennials. It's a reminder that despite spending the majority of our time meticulously crafting our online personas, we still have vital organs that need to be taken care of and family members we should probably interact with. More than anything, it's a reminder of the world we were introduced to the day we left our mothers' wombs. Those brave women didn't push us out of their vaginas just so we could strive to be interesting online and disconnected in the real world.

For me, it's more complicated than spending too much time on the Internet and not enough time focusing on what's going to get me ahead in life . . . because the Internet *is* what's getting me ahead in life. It's a strange dynamic, especially because when you work in the online space, people expect you to be someone who's always plugged in and spewing insights about how to make it in the modern world. And for a while, I felt an obligation to be that Internet version of myself at all times.

The struggle to live a life that looks as effortless as the life portrayed on social media is draining. It's no secret that the glimpses of our lives we show online aren't a completely honest portrayal of our actual lives. One of the most popular photos I ever posted on Instagram is of Steve Buscemi and me at a movie premiere. We're all smiles and the caption reads, "Hanging out with Steve Buscemi." You'd think we were best buddies and that he invites me to his Super Bowl party every year. The truth is that earlier in the night, Steve caught me staring at him in the bathroom while he was using the urinal. He shot me a disapproving look and walked out as quickly as he could. It wasn't until later in the night that I caught up with him and practically forced him to pose half-heartedly for a picture. But did my followers know that? Of course not—that might have hurt my chance of getting more likes.

My fear is that the tendency to perfect our self-image on social media ends up bleeding too much into our IRL existence. Sure, I've got things pretty put together in some areas of my life, but that doesn't mean I'm not knee-deep in personal issues, insecurities, and confusion. When I tried to push those less picturesque realities under the rug and exist only as an Instagram-worthy version of myself, I started to feel like maybe I'd lost touch with who I was.

For me, this book is a confessional. It's a reflection on the times I've displayed my weirdest tendencies and made borderline regrettable decisions, both on the Internet and offline. It's a collage of uncertainties and a collection of the moments that haven't been glamorous and predictable, because those are the moments I've learned from the most. Life (and especially my life) is awkward and confusing and full of bad sex and spilled coffee, and we shouldn't just throw a pretty filter over those memories. When we neglect those imperfect moments, we miss a chance for real growth.

I personally don't think there's anything wrong with keeping our social-media feeds as a highlight reel to look back on. But we owe it to ourselves to own up to the fact that we don't have every aspect of our lives—from our beautifully plated breakfast to our relationships and work life—figured out every single day. It's easy for me to tell someone to work hard and remain patient, that it will pay off eventually. The truth is, though, that I spend most of my time overanalyzing everything I do, as you'll soon find out. Life, after all, is a lot easier online than it is offline.

If life is indeed all about balance, then it's important to embrace the imperfect and the strange. If we lose that personal honesty, then whom exactly are we living for—ourselves or everyone else? Who knows, maybe it'll always be a bit of both. I'm still trying to figure that out, one step, click, swipe, and text at a time.

Or maybe someone out there is close to discovering a way for us to live inside our computers for the rest of time. In the event that happens, forget everything I just said.

People of the Internet, You Are Not Alone

I spend nearly every single day on Google Analytics for my job. Google Analytics is a service provided by Google that tracks everything possible to know about a website's traffic. A large portion of my time is dedicated to analyzing Elite Daily readers: tracking how many people visit the site, the cities they live in, how many articles they read, how long they read them for, whether they're male or female, young or old. The list goes on and on. I often have so many charts and numbers on my screen that if a stranger were to see me working, they'd assume I was in finance. But the numbers have nothing to do with budgets or yearly revenue; each one, instead, represents a person, living and breathing, completely unaware that I care so much about their existence, habits, and interests.

Attracting people to a website shares similarities with the techniques used by pick-up artists. You begin to learn and understand peoples' behaviors, or at least you try to. You start tracking what piques their interests as a collective group and what makes them come back for more. There's predictability to human behavior that often goes unseen, but when you search for it, and most of all, when you use it to your advantage, people become one rhythmic, faceless mass, almost like a wave, swaying and growing and shifting, just asking to be tamed and given what they want—even before they know it's what they want.

It's the job of any website to determine what stories its audience wants to read and share, and why. How do they want these stories delivered to them? What's the best time to deliver them? Do they like their titles long or short? Do they prefer pictures to be tall or wide?

Admittedly, there is a semispoken-but-mostly-unspoken truth across the digital media industry that working for the Internet will make you jaded. The consistent goal of driving people to a website can make you forget that those same people are more than just numbers that are tracked on a screen and tallied up in pretty graphs at the end of each month. It's not a life-altering jadedness that makes you incapable of human contact, but it does cause you to spend your morning commute viewing the people around you as potential clicks and page views. Each person a potential set of new eyes. Another visitor for the books.

Viewing people as statistics is nothing new in any business, especially media. The realization didn't leave me contemplating my purpose in life or whether or not I should quit my job. It's simply part of the game, and besides, it's rewarding to know you have the ability to influence so many people at one time, even if you'll never know them on a personal level. More than anything, the feeling of being disconnected—while at the same time connecting with millions of people online—is a side effect that lingers. It never quite festers and worsens. But I still found myself wishing for a way to find a hint of humanity in the numbers I tracked each day.

Enter the most interesting discovery I've made while working at Elite Daily, or while using the Internet period. Technically, I didn't discover it—Kaitlyn, the site's editor in chief, first showed it to me. And the timing couldn't have been better. Despite my borderline obsessive relationship with Google Analytics, I'd never paid attention to one function, a small, hardly noticeable feature labeled Top Keywords. Since Google provides the analytics service, the feature is able to show all the top searches that people typed into the Google search engine that, one way or another, led them to Elite Daily. Say you type a question like "Who's running for president?" or "Why do hangovers hurt so badly?" into the Google search box. Then say that Google search yields many results, including an Elite Daily article that could potentially answer your question. You click on that article, and suddenly, your initial question appears on my screen in the top-keywords page on Google Analytics. Pretty simple. Also pretty spy-like.

Kaitlyn first stumbled upon the feature after noticing a seemingly random list of questions while playing around with Google Analytics: hard-to-miss questions like "How do I change the taste of my vagina?" and "How to make her have sex with her ex-boyfriend?" She clicked into the top-keywords page and was greeted by a slew of similarly straightforward and unashamed questions and phrases that people all over the world were typing into their computers. The questions people were throwing into the Internet void were perfect combinations of vulgar, honest, and intensely private thoughts. She shared her discovery with me and we laughed like children, mostly at the fact that the bizarre searches were somehow leading back to Elite Daily.

Later that night, back at my apartment, I couldn't help but log on to Google Analytics for another dose of the top-keyword searches. I convinced myself I could use a laugh and decided I'd collect a few of the funniest searches to show Kaitlyn in the morning. In the darkness of my apartment, clicking into the keyword page felt like entering an AOL chat room my parents warned me to avoid as a child.

Immediately, the real-time keyword searches populated my screen:

How to enjoy my single life as a girl
After many sex lady vagina are loose why?
Human that make sex everyday

Difference in red and white wine
Do I smoke too much pot
How to become famous
How to pee with morning wood

Seeing the keywords refreshing every few seconds made the whole thing feel wrong and dangerous. I felt like a secret agent with access to strangers' most personal thoughts. Granted, I had no way of finding out who any of these people were or where they were located in the world, but the unknown made the whole operation feel even more scandalous.

Suddenly feeling like I was seeing too much, I shut my laptop. But five minutes later I was back on, watching the searches refresh like a stockbroker eyeing the market. I'd take screenshots of my favorites and before I knew it I had a folder full of them.

20 signs she is horny and wants to have sex
Does he qualify as an asshole

I felt powerful. I felt like the keeper of some great secret. I was obsessed.

It was the greatest form of entertainment I'd found in some time. The directness of some of the questions—many of them sexual, because, let's face it, all we think about is sex—were perfect in their delicate conciseness. They were written out exactly the way people thought them. Naturally, these sex questions were often the most absurd and humorous. Some of the more interesting searches included

Girls favorite penis

How many types of orgasms do we have

How do girls feel during periods

Effects of small penis during sex

Can your vagina be loose when you don't have a child

Great sex with screams

Does a hairy guy perform better in bed

How to know person masturbates

Desire to lick woman ass

Corkscrew penis

Can you get stuck together during sex

Someone out there in the world is truly curious whether or not you can tell if a person masturbates just by looking at him or her. What about the person wondering if hairy guys are good in bed? Is it a hairy guy who wants to know, or someone considering sleeping with a hairy guy? How hairy are we talking? We won't even address the corkscrew penis.

The narratives I conceived about the mysterious figures on the other end of the screen were endless. In my mind I was putting faces to the people I'd never know. Then there was the tantalizing thought that maybe, by some chance, out of the two billion people who use the Internet, one of the phrases I'd come across was written by someone I knew.

It was easy to be initially drawn to the vulgarity of the sex searches, but after some time I realized that a whole different layer of searches was far more delicate and humane. The first nonsexual question to catch my eye was "Can you fall in love with someone through texts." For some reason the words floored me. They jumped off the screen like poetry. I wanted to print the question on T-shirts and sell them in college parking lots. I wanted scientists to actually determine whether or not you could fall in love through texts. I wanted to write a thesis paper on it. I wanted to sell the words to Taylor Swift so she could use them as the title of her next song. I wondered how many of us have thought the same thing about texting before, too afraid to ask the question out loud. After noticing the "fall in love through text" question, I went on the hunt for similar questions, potent in their simplicity and sincerity. I quickly came across "How to hold hands with a guy" and "He said I love you too soon." The new screenshots I took felt personal, and the entire procedure became more than just an entertaining way to pass the time. Hints of genuine uncertainty shone through these new searches, and for the first time I realized my prayers to be more connected with Elite Daily's audience had been answered. Here was an entirely new look at readers as their most authentic selves—something flashing numbers on a screen could never reveal. You hear that people are their most honest selves when they think nobody is looking, and the Internet proves it. I cherished the new additions to my collection:

How to move forward with life

I cheated and I want to do it again

How to go from being a side chick to a girlfriend

Can't talk to girl I like

When a girl says sure what does it mean

Do women love men with belly

Am I a bad kisser

Can't get my girl to cuddle me

I like wearing socks during sex why?

Are guys without girlfriends useless

Boyfriend distant

How to keep your girl happy with words

Everyone else is getting married

Wife not adventurous with sex

I always get drunk and regret it

I felt more connected with the vast Internet population than ever before. Each day I'd wake up to a stream of strangers' most important life questions and concerns. It was like knowing the plots to countless movies but never being able to see the ending. I'd go through the day wondering whether that guy ended up getting his girlfriend to cuddle. Did the person who cheated end up cheating again? Did their partner find out?

If there's a lesson in any of this, it's that you are not alone, good people of the Internet. I saw so many questions repeated countless times, the most frequent (perhaps unsurprisingly) being those about sex, love, and family. We're all asking the same questions at some point in our lives, and there is something genuinely comforting in that.

Of course, you can have too much of a seemingly good thing. I was working from home the day it occurred to me that perhaps I'd taken advantage of the keyword feature's purpose. The truth is I'd gone a little too hard the night before, which happened to be a Tuesday. (Fun fact: Finishing a full bottle of sake by yourself pretty much guarantees you'll be working from home the following day.) After sleeping through my alarm, I logged online around 10 a.m., still too dizzy to pour my dehydrated self a glass of water. About twenty minutes into trying to get work done, I realized I'd be kidding myself if I thought it'd be a productive day. So I logged on to Google Analytics and headed straight to the keyword searches. At least it was sort of work related.

Through the haze of my hangover, I scanned the familiar list as it refreshed every few seconds. After a few refreshes I noticed a couple of distinctively somber searches. They especially stood out within the mix of the more common "how to give a blowjob" and "when to ask her out" questions.

Within seconds of one another I came across the following searches:

I hate people
Alone in the world

I was experiencing one of those overly dramatic hangovers in which you consider everything you've done in your life and whether it's all been worthwhile, so those searches hit me hard. I'd logged on to be cheered up by strangers of the Internet, not depressed by them. More than that, though, I had a hard time believing these heartbreakingly honest searches were a sudden, new trend. I'd never noticed questions like them, though. It occurred to me that I'd never really watched the searches unfold for long periods of time. I mostly just popped in and out throughout the day to grab a screenshot or two. It's possible that I'd conditioned myself to see what I wanted to see, collecting not the full spectrum of searches, but whatever pleased my mood. When I hoped to find funny sex questions, it seemed like there was an abundance of funny sex questions. When I was on the prowl for poetic confessions like "Can you fall in love through texts," the supply seemed endless.

Since there was no chance of my moving from the couch, I decided I'd keep an eye on the searches. Throughout the next couple of hours, there was mostly a stream of the usual types of questions about love and sex and how to save money, though in between those, I pulled out "Feeling depressed need help," "Is it normal to constantly plan for death," and "Why did my mother have to die."

Combined with my pounding headache and a lingering taste of acidic regret drying out my mouth, the searches only made me feel worse. Throughout the rest of the day I collected:

Trust issues with abusive mom

Husband is quiet and distant

Am I in love with someone I can never have

He will never love me back

Is there a point in living if she doesn't love me back

When you find out your man is cheating

I hate meeting people

Why do I think about suicide

Don't belong in my family

Doubt that people love me

When I was young I'd go camping every year with my dad and brother. We'd usually spend long weekends at a campground in Upstate New York, fishing during the day, sitting around a fire at night, and sleeping on the uneven ground in a tent. On most nights, my dad would want to go for a walk to get a better view of the stars. The walks always enticed me as much as they frightened me, mostly because the darkness that enveloped the campground at night was unlike any darkness

I'd known before. It was thick and had weight to it. Anything could have been hiding in that darkness and you'd never know. I was always conflicted during those walks. I wanted to use my flashlight, but at the same time, shining the light into the woods around us meant the possibility of revealing something I didn't want to see. At that age, a bustling imagination enhances the fear of the unknown. That fear usually resulted in my walking closely by my dad's side, following the single stream of light from his flashlight that illuminated the path ahead. It felt safe to let the darkness play its role, to let whatever was concealed by it stay that way.

By the end of the day, as my hangover was finally beginning to wind down, I felt like I'd been shining my flashlight places I shouldn't have. I'd always sensed that perhaps I was overstepping a boundary by taking pleasure in the private thoughts of others, and that fateful day proved my theory to be correct. Yes, nothing you do on the Internet is private, but I doubt people assume that means a twenty-five-year-old in Queens is collecting their most intimate thoughts in a folder on his MacBook. Regardless of the fact I didn't know who they were, a part of me was still finding joy in their genuine struggles. And clearly the searches weren't only coming from teens wondering how to hold hands and cuddle their girlfriends. They were from a range of people who had lost loved ones, were fighting depression, and were simply trying as hard as the rest of us to figure out their purpose in this sometimes lonely life.

I decided to give up the keywords feature cold turkey. I made a hungover vow to myself to let strangers' deep, personal Google searches float around the Internet cosmos without my interference. Besides, rather than spy on countless Elite Daily readers, I could do my actual job and make sure the site remained relevant.

If my admittedly strange obsession with reading the private thoughts of others had taught me anything, it's that we're all trying to cope with what life throws at us, whether it's good, bad, or somewhere in between. We're all asking ourselves questions we'd never ask out loud. The woman passing you by may be trying to figure out why her husband has been acting so distant. That woman who ruined your day by accidentally stepping on your new shoes could have just lost someone she loved. The guy sitting across from you could very well have a corkscrew penis.

During my morning commute, when I'm surrounded by tired-looking faces and people preparing for another day, I can only imagine the range of questions that a single subway car would yield if they were to appear on my computer screen. Now when I make eye contact with a stranger across a train car, I don't see them as a statistic. I don't even create fictional stories about them and their interests. I just smile to myself, finding comfort in the fact that the Internet is there for them, in all its anonymous and nonjudgmental glory.

Translation

I was thirty thousand feet in the air and halfway to Italy for a two-week trip with my family when the panic set in. It was the same panic I experience almost every time I travel internationally. It has nothing to do with turbulence and crying babies and everything to do with the fact that in a few short hours I'll be in a country that speaks an entirely different language from my own.

I gave up on my dream of learning another language a long time ago. For some reason, capturing even the basic phonetics of any foreign dialect is impossible for me, no matter how often I practice in the shower. Even pronouncing the names of wines has proven too difficult, so much so that I find myself ordering whatever's easiest to say out loud at restaurants and not what I actually want to drink. Despite all of this, I actually travel often, for both work and pleasure, so there's never a shortage of anxiety and embarrassment.

Surprisingly, I can recall a decent number of Spanish phrases from my high-school classes. The words even sound fluent when I say them in my head. But then I open my mouth and suddenly I'm yelling like a drunken game-show host, adding unnecessary emphasis to words in a voice much deeper than the one I use to speak English. I first realized this in Barcelona, when I asked a street vendor *"Cuanto dinero?"* for a pair of sunglasses and came off like I was announcing he'd just won a brand new car.

In Paris, I got by by mumbling *"bonjour"* and *"merci"* while walking as quickly as possible in the opposite direction of whomever I was spewing sound at. I got so good at the walk-and-talk that locals and cashiers started calling after me in French to strike up conversations, assuming, I imagine, that someone in such a hurry couldn't possibly be a tourist. In South Africa, people were prepared to perform the Heimlich maneuver on me when I attempted to pronounce *"goeie môre,"* which is Afrikaans for good morning. In Brazil, my *"obrigado"* rolled off my tongue with an embarrassing bravado that sounded nothing like Portuguese and more like an exaggerated line from an Italian mob boss in *The Godfather*. One time in Belize, a tour guide tried to teach me how to properly enunciate the phrase, "Me belly full," which is a way to suggest "I've had enough to eat" in Belizean Creole. What should have resembled an accent similar to Jamaican Patois squeaked out of me the way I imagine leprechauns sing.

Now when I travel, I'm fine up until the point the trip starts to feel real, which is around the same time I realize I can't fall asleep on the plane or a flight attendant crushes my elbow with a beverage cart. Then the fear of embarrassing myself takes over, and suddenly the trip I'd been anticipating becomes the trip I'm dreading.

I realized midflight that Italy was intimidating me more than any other country I'd been to, mostly because I've spent the majority of my life in America telling people I'm Italian. Americans love to ask anyone and everyone "what they are," even when they know that person's ancestry has played little to no part in their upbringing. My answer to this question has always been, "I'm mostly Italian." I'm Italian only on my mother's side, but her family is more than double the size of my father's, so I grew up eating pasta on Sundays and hearing stories about my great-grandmother cutting the heads off live chickens in the kitchen. That's Italian enough for me. Or at least in America it is.

Being of Italian descent in America, like being of any ethnic descent in America, doesn't automatically mean you've lived some wildly different life than anyone else around you. Unless you're first or maybe second generation, odds are you grew up similarly to the people around you who were the same age. Other than the selection of home-cooked meals and the religion my parents raised me in, my childhood wasn't all that different than the Puerto Rican kids down the road or the Jewish kid across the street.

Of the people I've met whose answer to the "what are you" question is also an apprehensive "Italian," most don't speak any Italian in their homes or have family members living in Italy. For many, being Italian in America is an excuse to buy meats from a privately owned deli with a name like Roscoe's or Carmine's Pork Store, because supermarkets can't possibly import their sausage and salami the same way. The closest my family comes to speaking Italian is pronouncing the names of foods in illogical ways. *Mozzarella* is "mutts-a-dell," *prosciutto* somehow becomes "bro-shoot," and *gnocchi* is a completely new word each time.

In 2009, the reality of being a modern-day Italian American was exploited and exaggerated on the show *Jersey Shore*, and on all the embarrassing seasons and spin-offs that followed. Suddenly being Italian American was like being in an artificially tan, gym-worshipping, vodka-guzzling cult. The problem was that the show's participants truly believed, or were paid to truly believe, that attributes like loyalty, hospitality, and friendship were strictly reserved for Italian Americans—as if they weren't familial and even basic human traits. Perhaps that's the beauty of the confused Italian American clan: they take genuine pride in and ownership of characteristics that are universal.

Most likely, the show was just a last stand to depict the average white American as something cooler and more exotic than your average white American. In turn, white people became that much more uncool and infinitely less exotic.

For me, traveling to Italy meant finally experiencing the culture I'd half-assed and blindly considered my own. I turned to my brother, Cole, and proposed we pretend to be Dutch or English, even though he was in honors Italian in high school at the time. We even brushed up on what we remembered from sign-language classes we'd taken. Anything to avoid being exposed as the pasta-eating frauds we felt we were.

When we finally landed and ventured out in Rome, not attempting to speak Italian was easy. Like most big cities around the world, there are so many tourists and transplants that it's easier if everyone just uses broken English. Even Americans use broken English when traveling abroad. We can't help but shout fragmented sentences like "Pizza, how much?" and "Bathroom? Toilet? Where?" Things just seem more efficient this way. And as long as you're adequately apologetic and defeated, the Romans are cool with it, too.

My mother, whose maiden name is Visceglia and whose ancestors hail from Bari, a small coastal town in southern Italy, had been planning this great return to the motherland for some time. It was the kind of vacation that a family talks about for so many years that it seems like it's never going to happen, until one day it just does. The kind of vacation for which people cash in years' worth of saved-up coins.

From Rome we traveled to Florence and from Florence to Siena. We moved quickly through each city, taking in the sights, filling up on carbohydrates, and staring at gelato behind glass as if each flavor were a relic from Jesus's childhood laid out neatly on display. Like in Rome, we defaulted to English, minus my mother's few painful attempts at "*grazie*." She spent a full year prior to the trip listening to Italian language-learning audio guides in her car, but somehow her limited vocabulary sounded more like Arabic than anything else. It's clear whose genes I got in the foreign-language department. After enough glasses of wine my father would resort to the Spanish he knew, throwing out "*gracias*" left and right and, I'm pretty sure, an "*adios*" or two. Cole refused to speak a word of Italian, despite my mother's insistent requests. I opened my mouth only to eat.

We spent a full week hopping from city to city, and the plan for the second week was to rent a car and head to the mountains, away from the bustling tourism. My mother's dream had always been to spend a week in a villa in Tuscany . . . or it had at least been her dream since seeing the movie *Under the Tuscan Sun*. Something tells me a lot of middle-aged women have the same dream, but good for her for acting on it. The only difference is most women probably dream of leaving their husbands then traveling to a villa in Italy. Good for her for not acting on that.

The deeper into the mountains we drove, the less English the locals spoke. Somewhere along the way to Caprese Michelangelo, where the villa was located, we took a wrong turn onto a narrow, cobblestoned road and our car ended up in a dead-end alley. When we rolled down the window and asked three older ladies passing by if they could help us with directions, they looked at us in awe, as if our car were a spaceship and they were the first humans to make contact with extraterrestrials. More likely, we were the first English speakers to ever make it that far into the mountains.

Thanks to some crafty maneuvering, we eventually got the car out of the alley and continued up the terrifying and steep mountain roads toward the villa. There weren't many homes or people along the way, just a few scattered churches and endless green fields. It turns out Caprese Michelangelo was the birthplace of the artist Michelangelo. I stared out the window on the way up the mountain, trying to see where his inspiration may have come from, while at the same time praying we didn't hit a turn too fast that would send us plummeting to our deaths.

Thankfully, we made it to our destination in one piece. As we inched our way up the winding driveway, I was surprised by the villa's modest stature and underwhelming appearance. It's not that the place wasn't nice, but there's definitely a certain expectation attached to the word *villa*. The word calls to mind images of luxury and wealth. A villa, in my mind, was a place where rich people go to feel even richer without having to interact with humans other than the ones they handpick.

About twenty cats were waiting outside upon our arrival, like some sort of mangy welcome brigade. They all took turns rubbing their alarmingly skinny bodies against our legs as we made our way to the front door and wondered if Italian cats had fleas. We had to squeeze through the door one by one to make sure none of the emaciated animals made it into the house. Once we were all inside we dropped our bags, turned to each other while letting out a sigh of relief, then simultaneously asked, "What is that smell?"

The entire place smelled like death, or shit, or someone who took a shit all over the place before dying. It didn't take long to figure out it was coming from the nearest bathroom—it was impossible to get close to the door without gagging. It was as if Michelangelo himself had taken a dump and forgotten to flush, and we were the first people in history to stumble upon it.

I looked at my mother, her shirt over her nose, eyes teary from the stench, and wondered if her dream of a pleasant Italian villa was already tarnished. Then there was a knock at the door. It was the woman we'd rented the house from. Her name was Marianella and she lived with her family in a small house no more than two hundred feet from our villa. They owned the entire property. Aside from the villa and their house, there was a tiny, rundown church and a fully functioning farm on the premises, complete with cows, sheep, roosters, pigs, and a barn, all no more than a short walk away. Rome and Florence and all the other busy cities with their McDonald's restaurants and broken English and lines for museums felt like they were on the opposite side of the world. We were farm people now, with a bathroom that reeked of the apocalypse and twenty starving cats waiting outside our front door.

Marianella entered the house and we immediately pointed to the bathroom while waving our hands in front of our noses, which is the international sign for "your villa smells like sewage, please do something immediately." She quickly caught on and began frantically mumbling Italian words to herself. It was clear she didn't speak a word of English, not even *hi*. Somehow my mother had been able to book our stay through a bare-bones, poorly translated website she stumbled upon. As Marianella made her way to the bathroom, still mumbling frantically, I couldn't help but feel guilty, like the mess was somehow our fault. I imagined she was muttering something like, "Stupid Americans need everything to be perfect. If anyone else had rented the villa they wouldn't have minded the smell. Don't they realize it's part of the experience? It pairs nicely with the starving cats and farm animals. I bet these are those types of Americans who call themselves Italian. They don't know the first thing about being Italian. Their pasta's not al dente."

Assuming foreigners are cynical, judgmental, American-hating monsters is another of my insecurities that comes to light when I travel. Traveling is like a good therapist; it can take the most confident people and bring them far enough outside their comfort zone that they start to realize all the uncertainties they have about themselves. Too often, when I return home from a trip, I find myself wondering if spending so much time trying to make myself invisible caused me to miss out on an even greater experience, or if I missed some great pictures because I was worried it would look "touristy" if I took my camera out.

I did some research on the anxiety I feel on trips, and a number of searches led me to *xenophobia*, which is an unreasonable fear of things that are foreign or strange. The key word being *unreasonable*. Though what I feel is more like reverse xenophobia: an unreasonable fear that I will appear too foreign and strange. Basically, I'm afraid of appearing awkward as fuck in a country that's not my own. Is there a word for that?

When Marianella was finally finished assessing the situation, she talked directly to us. We watched her as if she were a character on a screen and the subtitles weren't working. Then Cole, who hadn't spoken a word of Italian all trip, stepped forward and started talking. Marianella's face lit up. She was probably wondering why the person who knew some Italian had been quiet the entire time. The two of them exchanged choppy dialogue for a few minutes, smiling in agreement when they'd finally understand what the other was saying.

Eventually Marianella waved good-bye and headed out the front door as quickly as she'd entered. We turned to Cole for an explanation.

"I think she said someone will fix the bathroom by tomorrow," he explained. "And she invited us to their house for dinner tonight. Everything in town is closed."

Dinner, of all things, is the most important part of being Italian American. The kitchen table is the most sacred place in the home, and no, you may not be excused early. A part of me wanted to be excited for the invite, but at the same time all my fears culminated in this very kind invitation. Not only could I not communicate with these people, but now they had the chance to judge my American ignorance in their own home. This was on top of the fact that everything I thought I knew about being Italian was probably going to be proven wrong.

Later that night we made the long-awaited trek from our shit-scented villa to the house. It was a short walk up a narrow half-dirt, half-stone path. Marianella and her husband Francesco greeted us. They didn't quite say hello. Their greeting was more of a barrage of sound mixed with firm handshakes from Francesco, who had a thick beard and hands that were permanently dirty from years of farming. They led us into their kitchen where they introduced their two daughters, Martina and Francesca (Yes, Francesco named one of his daughters Francesca).

Francesco pointed to the kitchen table and we all sat. It was strange going through the motions of dinner without any real dialogue. It felt like a holiday dinner when you get stuck at a table with old people you don't really know. My concerns were to sit up straight, smile, and make no sudden movements. I felt the weight of America's reputation on my shoulders. We tried passing phrases like "your house is lovely" and "what a beautiful family" through Cole. As he searched for the words, Marianella sliced her finger open while cutting up food and spent the next five minutes apologizing, continuing to prepare dinner in spite of what looked like a deep wound.

After wrapping a paper towel around her cut finger, Francesco left the room and came back with an actual pig leg. "Prosciutto," he announced, plopping the fresh leg directly on the table. Marianella poured us all glasses of wine, the paper towel on her finger stained red with blood. As Francesco began to cut the pig leg into delicious-looking slices of pro-sciutto, Cole, who was a vegetarian at the time, explained in his best Italian that he did not eat meat. The look that came over Francesco's face was one of disgust and confusion. His eyes locked onto Cole's and after a few seconds he responded in a flustered tone. Cole turned to us. "He said it's not meat, it's prosciutto." Martina and Francesca put their heads in their palms. They'd been sighing to themselves the entire time, clearly embarrassed by their parents, but unwilling to speak up. It made me more comfortable that they were as noticeably anxious as I was.

Eventually Francesco understood that Cole wouldn't eat the prosciutto and cooked him eggs straight from the farm. As we ate, Cole did his best to hold together the conversation between us, but he struggled to create real dialogue. It was Martina who eventually thought to turn on the computer and try out an online translator. Suddenly, all things were possible. The translations weren't spot on, but we could at least ask questions and provide general answers. Cole and Martina took turns typing and translating. We'd all wait in silence at the table for the translation to process before erupting in unison, delayed, but just as engaged as if we were conversing in real time. We spoke about everything from taxes to food to school. I was a college student at the time, and when I had Cole type "I study English" into the computer, they were impressed that I didn't know any other languages but was so passionate about the one I did know. My dad's job, which is head nurse of an operating room, translated to plastic surgeon. He happily went along with it.

After making our way through a few complete conversations, we were finally able to relax and be ourselves. We were poorly translated versions of ourselves, but we were ourselves nonetheless. At the very least, we were able to brush off the assumptions we'd come to the table with and appreciate that we had so much in common. Even Francesca and Martina joined in the conversation. We ended up speaking for hours, not realizing time was passing so quickly. Looking back, it's difficult to even remember the computer being present. In my memory, the conversation flowed as naturally as any I've ever had.

When we finished the wine, Francesco poured us all grappa he'd made in his backyard. It tasted like gasoline and a hint of death, but that didn't stop us from toasting to family and new friends. Yes, the pasta they served was cooked to al dente perfection and the wine may as well have been God's tears in a bottle, but I felt right at home. We were just two families having dinner, finding common ground over food, wine, and laughter.

The next day, the smell in the bathroom was gone, just as Marianella had promised. We spent the rest of the week relaxing by the pool and taking mental photographs of our view of Tuscany's rolling green mountains and olive trees. We had stumbled upon a little slice of paradise after all. We were invited back to one more dinner during our stay, and it was just as enjoyable as the first. Francesco even gave us a bottle of grappa to bring home. When it was finally time to say good-bye, I felt like I was leaving people I'd known for much longer than one week and surely not people I had at one point hoped to avoid at all costs.

Now, when I travel to new countries, I try my hardest to shake off any anxiety that creeps into my system. I still can't pronounce foreign words correctly for the life of me, but I'm starting to realize that's nothing to be all that ashamed of. If I ever do find myself consumed with a familiar fear of being too foreign and strange, either at home or abroad, I think of the dinner in Italy. More specifically, the moment I came to terms with the fact that being awkward and embarrassing is just part of being human.

Maybe one day Francesco, Marianella, and their two daughters will travel to America and eat at my family's dinner table.

I'm sure they'd have a ton of fears and insecurities while visiting a new country for the first time. If that day ever does come, I'll be sure to tell them, in my best Italian, *Siamo tutti estranei da qualche parte.*

"We're all strangers someplace."

Seeking an Underwear Expert

When I was ten years old I made the change from tighty-whities to boxer shorts. It was a transition that changed the world as I knew it. What was once uncomfortably held captive in a prison of fabric could now roam freely. A few years later I discovered boxer briefs, and once again my universe was turned upside down. Unlike its free-spirited cousin, the boxer short, boxer briefs offered actual support. Where tighty-whities would suffocate and cling, the boxer brief allowed enough room to breathe while still providing reinforcement. My discovery of boxer briefs was the first time I saw hope for nuance in a world that, as a middle-school student in suburbia, was overwhelmingly clear-cut. Life up to that point had been a matter of black or white, right or wrong, too much support or none at all. Boxer briefs opened my eyes to the gray area of life. A perfect balance between too much and too little existed after all.

After my decision to go through life wearing boxer briefs, I stopped thinking about underwear altogether. The first time the subject crossed my mind again wasn't until I was twenty-two and had been living on my own for six months. I received a call from my boss at the small website I was writing for and listened as he explained that he wasn't able to raise enough money to continue operations. In short, I was out of luck. One moment I had a job and the next I was unemployed, wondering for the first time ever how I'd pay the next month's rent. The thought of moving back in with my parents became a terrifyingly real possibility. They had warned me that my job wasn't secure enough to move out, but that had only pushed me to get my own place sooner.

Up until the moment my boss called, I had been living my childhood dream of having an apartment in New York City and supporting myself through writing. The paychecks weren't spectacular, but I was able to work from home. I didn't even have to change out of my pajamas (or my boxer briefs) if I didn't want to. Best of all, I could call myself a professional writer. It didn't matter that I was writing two-hundred-word articles on obscure bands I'd never heard of for a website nobody read. I was getting paid for my craft and that made me a professional.

I'd become so obsessed with finally being a paid writer that doing anything other than writing wasn't an option. Immediately after the call, I went online to find a new writing opportunity. I scoured Craigslist for hours, sending my resume to just about anyone willing to exchange actual money for words. That's when I came across the job listing for a "talented writer interested in covering the exciting men's underwear scene." I hadn't even realized men's underwear had a scene. It was late, but I decided there was no harm in sending out one more resume.

For the next week, the only e-mails I woke up to were motivational quotes from my mother and spam urging me to order the latest groundbreaking male enhancement pill, guaranteed to work or my money back. Then one morning, a reply to one of the hundreds of jobs I'd applied for appeared in my inbox. The subject line read "Seeking an Underwear Expert." The e-mail explained that the leading men's underwear website on the Internet was looking for someone to review newly released underwear. There was no actual website given, but Bobby, the mystery man behind the e-mail, assured me that I'd be given all the details during the in-person interview the following Wednesday.

I was certainly no expert on underwear. I couldn't even name three brands. All I knew was that the underwear ads that appeared in magazines and on billboards were perfectly photographed and positioned so that anyone passing by couldn't escape the ever-present, giant bulge, similar to how the *Mona Lisa*'s eyes always follow you around. With my minimal funds running lower each day and no other prospects on the horizon, I decided to take the interview. I imagined that there was a Hemingway quote floating around somewhere that went something like, "A good writer can fake being an expert in any-thing—even men's underwear."

On the morning of my interview I found myself in a staring contest with my underwear drawer. I couldn't help but think there'd be a test upon arrival. Perhaps an underwear check at the door, and they'd only allow me inside if I were wearing a worthy pair. I pushed aside the generic-brand boxer briefs and dug for the Calvin Kleins I'd picked up somewhere along the way. I didn't even know if Calvin Klein underwear was popular. I would have checked the website to find out, but I had no idea what it was, or more importantly, if it really existed.

If there were to ever be a mass human-trafficking ring set up through Craigslist it would most likely be disguised as a job interview for a men's underwear website. But the combination of needing money and a burning desire to work my way up in my chosen career of writing made me take my chances.

When I arrived at the address given in the e-mail I was sur-prised to see there were no office buildings around. Instead I stood directly in front of a luxury residential building on the lower West Side of Manhattan that overlooked the Hudson River. It was the kind of apartment building I'd only ever seen on commercials for *The Real Housewives of New York City*. I con-sidered turning around and going home. Anything can happen behind closed apartment doors. People die in their apartments and aren't found until weeks later, when neighbors start com-plaining about a peculiar smell. I didn't want mine to be one of the bodies found when the police finally raided the luxurious slaughter den of New York City's elusive underwear killer.

After taking a lap around the block to clear my head I decided to push forward and at least see what the inside of the building looked like. Before heading in I called my roommate and told him my exact location along with strict instructions to call the police and my parents, in that order, if he didn't hear from me in an hour. If anything were to happen I at least had on my best pair of underwear.

Inside the building I was greeted by a doorman and gave the name Bobby had told me to say. The doorman looked me up and down before telling me the floor and apartment number and pointing in the direction of an elevator. "Come check on me in twenty minutes," I wanted to say before heading off alone into the unknown.

In front of the apartment door I took a deep breath and knocked. A young man, who looked no older than twenty-five and had brightly dyed blonde hair, answered the door.

"Greg!" he shouted with familiarity, as if he'd known me for years.

"Bobby?" I asked, and he nodded.

He led me into the apartment and my jaw hit the floor. The ceiling was at least the height of a professional basketball hoop, which is the only way I am able to effectively judge the height of anything. A white bear rug, the kind that only exists in catalogues and cartoons, was sprawled across the hardwood floor.

Glass vases lined a marble fireplace mantle and floor-to-ceiling windows overlooked downtown Manhattan and the river. The walls were painted mostly grey and black, which made the white furniture and accents pop like budding flowers all over the room. There was a white leather couch, thick white fashion books on an all-glass table, a white leather chair, and an abstract white ceramic statue on a circular black table. I felt like I was in a *Vogue* photo shoot and couldn't help but wonder why there wasn't a model lying across the bear rug, running her fingers through her hair and biting her lower lip.

"You could fit a basketball hoop in here," I told Bobby.

"I know, right?" He laughed. "Nicholas isn't one for sports though. Let me go get him and tell him you're here."

I had no idea who Nicholas was, though I made a mental note to not break the ice with a sports reference. I took a seat on the white leather couch and waited.

Nicholas emerged suddenly from another room and made his way directly to the white leather chair adjacent to the couch. He sat down immediately and crossed his legs. I stood up to shake his hand and give him my resume. He denied the piece of paper and explained that he's not one for overexamining a person's exaggerated job history.

Where Bobby had been warm and welcoming, Nicholas was cold and stoic. He was wearing a perfectly fitted blue suit that looked as if it were painted on his thin frame. He wore round, wire-thin glasses, and from where I was sitting on the couch when he first walked in, he too looked as if he could be as tall as a basketball hoop. He was at least ten years older than Bobby and his exceptionally groomed facial hair made me feel insecure about the stubble I left sprinkled on my face to appear older and more seasoned.

"This is a great place," I told him.

"Thanks, it's home," he answered as quickly as the words could leave his mouth. Then he added, "So what do you know about my website?"

"Well there was no website given in the e-mail," I noted, second-guessing whether or not I'd missed the link when reading Bobby's response to my application.

"So then you aren't familiar with it is what you're saying? What are you familiar with, Greg?"

I got the sense that Nicholas was the type of employer who really enjoyed the interview process. Not so much as a process to gain an understanding of the person being interviewed, but more so as a way to exert authority and weed out candidates with pointed, uncomfortable questions. Admittedly, it had always been a dream of mine to one day put my feet up during an interview and throw out obscure questions to a nervous recent graduate sitting across from me with a stack of their own freshly printed resumes that I refused to look at. I always fantasized about asking an interviewee questions like "What's your spirit animal?" and "If you could eat only one food that you've never tasted before for the rest of your life, what would it be?"

The number of questions with no right answers are endless. If that was the game Nicholas was after, then I had no choice but to wow him with my answers.

"I'm familiar with great writing, creativeness, and passion, and I know that's what I can offer you," I responded. He perked up in his chair, then asked the question I knew was coming all along: "Why underwear, Greg?"

I looked around the apartment one more time, taking in all the extravagant home goods and furniture I'd never seen before in real life. If that was what caring about underwear could get a person, then underwear was what I'd dedicate myself to.

I don't remember most of what I said, but the opening line of my response was, "Because underwear is at the core of every man." From there I spoke about how underwear, unlike other fashion items, is the first and last article of clothing a man interacts with in his day. I added that like a man, underwear could be so many things at once; soft and comfortable, yet sturdy and ready for whatever grueling tasks may come along. It was shocking how quickly I was able to throw the false sentiments together and how many metaphors came pouring out of me. It must have worked because Nicholas stood up and asked me to follow him into the other room.

He pulled two chairs up to a desk with a computer on it and asked me to join him in taking a look at the website. Bobby brought us bottles of sparkling water from the kitchen and set them down on two white coasters. It was clear Nicholas had loosened up almost immediately after my impromptu under-wear monologue.

"You're going to love the design," he said, giddy for the page to load.

Once the website loaded we were greeted by a large image of an oiled-up man with a ripped six-pack and nothing on except for a type of underwear I'd never seen. The back resembled a woman's thong and the front looked like the mesh bags high-school gym teachers use to carry around balls. As Nicholas scrolled through the site, more images appeared of chiseled men in underwear that looked like nothing I'd ever come across in stores. Some looked like speedos and others were practically see-through.

"A lot of images on the homepage," I said.

"Well you've got to give the men what they want," Nicholas responded. "Draw them in with the bulge then inform them of the style and fit." He laughed.

"The gist of the job," Bobby added, "is actually wearing and reviewing the underwear, but also writing feature stories, secur-ing interviews with the models, and sourcing the images."

My lack of immediate enthusiasm must have been obvious because Nicholas turned to me and asked, "You're gay, aren't you?" as bluntly as he'd posed his earlier questions.

Once again, my answer turned into something much more philosophical than it needed to be. I explained that I wasn't gay, but that the beauty of fashion, and especially men's underwear, is that it transcends gay or straight.

"But my cousin is gay and we talk about fashion and men's underwear all the time," I added at the end. The first part wasn't a lie, but my cousin and I have never had even one conversation about fashion, and certainly none about men's underwear.

I could see the concern on Nicholas's and Bobby's faces. "And you'd be okay with creating this kind of content and finding these kinds of pictures?" Nicholas asked.

I could have told him no and parted ways. If I had gotten any other responses to job applications that morning, I may have; but as it stood, I was days away from rent being due and had an opportunity in front of me. I was too afraid to say no. I looked Nicholas straight in the eyes and said, "Yes, completely comfortable." Besides, if I got the job, I could just tell people I was a men's fashion writer and never send them samples of my work.

I was sent back out to the white couch while Nicholas and Bobby deliberated in the other room. After a few minutes passed they came out and Nicholas threw a pair of black underwear in my direction.

"If you're really as interested in underwear as you seem to be, get me two hundred words on this pair by tomorrow afternoon. They're the new Under Armour briefs, not out on the market yet. Work out in them and make sure you sweat."

With that said, we shook hands and I was back out on the street, texting my roommate that I was not only alive, but the owner of underwear that had yet to be released to the public.

Back at my apartment I studied the underwear in my hands as if it were a Rubik's Cube, trying to figure out how to make its stitching and spandex-polyester blend sound sexy yet reliable. I spent most of the night writing and rewriting lines about the underwear's athletic and durable material and masculine waistband. I struggled to seamlessly use adjectives like bold and sleek. I looked up product descriptions of what I imagined to be similar underwear and assumed that the pair I was holding also had antiodor qualities and temperature-controlling fabric.

I tried the underwear on and paced around my room. I made sure to note that they didn't bunch up. The breathability seemed good as well. I was too nervous to take any time away from writing to actually work out in them, so I did a few push-ups and ran in place to get the effect.

I finally shut my laptop at around three in the morning. The two short paragraphs I had written haunted me as I tried to fall asleep. I'd jump up from bed every ten minutes or so to tweak a sentence about the mesh pouch or do more research on the purpose of stretch mobility. It was like forcing myself to speak a new language without knowing what any of the words meant.

In the morning I woke up groggy and dazed from the night spent staring deep into my computer screen. I immediately opened up my laptop to my underwear review. I read it over once and cringed at the words I'd thrown together. It wasn't that the review was poorly written. In fact, it sounded great, as if I really knew what I was talking about. This false authenticity made it even worse. After a night of realizing how much I disliked writing about underwear, I now felt like I was mocking Nicholas's passion by faking my knowledge about what he had built his professional life on.

I did some research on Nicholas and found that he'd started a number of successful fashion websites prior to his underwear venture. There were pictures of him with celebrities and models all over the Internet. He clearly knew what he was doing. You don't end up with a bear rug in your apartment by faking your way through life and pretending to be passionate about something as specific as men's underwear.

I closed out of my review and opened up Craigslist and a few other job-search sites. Their pages were filled with a ton of brand new listings since I'd looked a couple days ago. I then checked my funds and began crunching numbers. I realized that if I adhered to a strict-enough budget, I'd have just enough to pay the month's rent and shop sparingly at the grocery store. I'd be able to extend my job search by a week. Two if I gave up a meal a day. It was a risk, but it seemed more realistic than lying my way into a job I had no interest in. Besides, the painstaking hours it took just to make two paragraphs about a pair of underwear I knew nothing about sound authentic left my head spinning.

When I finally sat down to send an e-mail to Nicholas, I decided I'd be honest. I told him that after sleeping on it, I didn't feel I was the person he was looking for. I thanked him for the opportunity and the pair of really cool underwear I assumed he didn't want back. I also sent over the final version of the review I'd written and let him know that if there was anything worth using, he could.

I decided I'd go for a run to clear my head before diving back into job-search mode. Halfway out the door, I turned back and changed out of the boxers I had on and into the brand new pair I'd spent the night trying to get to know so intimately. I at least had to work out in them and sweat. I owed Nicholas that much.

Perhaps that made-up Hemingway quote isn't, "A good writer can fake being an expert in anything." Maybe instead, it's something more along the lines of, "A great writer knows when not to fake being an expert." Either way, underwear would remain to me what it had always been in my adult life: something hidden away in a drawer that I put on and took off and washed without a second thought.

#Mom

I always figured the day I started guiding my parents through life would come with old age, when one of them required a diaper or couldn't be trusted driving at night. But my mother jump-started the process with her interest in social media. I imagine she saw the closing window of opportunity to understand the world's new mode of communication and made the leap. It was either that or end up like the other half of her generation, driving to the post office twice a week to send something that could have easily been e-mailed. That's the path my father has chosen. His contacts will forever be a grueling and arduous phone call away, and not the click of a send button on Facebook.

When my fifty-three-year-old mother first attempted to use social media, it was as if she'd been handed a stack of textbooks written in hieroglyphics and asked to learn their contents. She had no idea where to begin, so she'd call me each night with a long list of questions, such as "What's the difference between twittering and tweeting?" or "Do I have to be friends with strangers on Facebook?" I'd go through the basics the best I could, though each call would end with my getting frustrated, and her getting frustrated that I was frustrated.

"I don't even know why I'm doing this," she'd groan. "It's stupid anyway."

We'd hang up on each other, agitated and fed up, knowing we'd pick up right where we left off the very next day.

"I don't know how you do it every week," I confessed to my girlfriend, Brittany, a kindergarten teacher. "I can't even handle a half hour."

Despite her frustrations, my mother would pull out her ancient-looking laptop each night and labor tirelessly over her digital identity. She'd sit in the same chair with one finger hovering hesitantly above the keyboard and her eyes scrunched behind reading glasses. My brother, Cole, would text me pictures and we'd laugh together at her struggles. It took her one full week to successfully create a Facebook account, and after all the effort, she forgot the password.

Eventually, she figured out how to set her profile picture and find friends. Marie Dybec was officially an online presence.

"But why isn't anybody liking my statuses?" she'd ask, genuinely hurt.

"In time they will," I'd assure her. "Babies don't come out running."

Soon, my mother's commitment paid off and she showed real progress. I called Cole in shock the day she tweeted her first hashtag.

"Did you teach her that?" I asked.

"No. She did it on her own!"

We were proud, the way parents must be that first time their kid poops in the toilet without help.

Within the next few months, my mother—the woman who once asked me if the Internet shuts off at night—was managing a personal Facebook page as well as one for her business, a beauty salon she's owned since she was twenty-three; a Twitter account with a hashtag in almost every tweet; and an Instagram account with a #throwbackthursday photo, guaranteed, each week.

What started as a stream of blurry pictures of the family dog had transformed into strategically taken selfies with captions like, "Woke up like this," and updates about "hanging with her bestie." My friends, mostly the girls, took notice.

"Your mom is, like, really living life in her twenties right now," Brittany noted one day. "She's kind of the perfect millennial."

My mother did seem to have more energy. Her jokes were getting funnier. She even acquired two gay best friends that taught my dad how to dance without leaving his stiff, Frankenstein arms at his side. It was as if my mother was growing younger before my eyes.

I was home for Thanksgiving the night she blurted out, "I'm such a hashtag slut." Cole and I nearly choked on our food. My father stood speechless behind us, thoroughly confused.

"My goal is twenty hashtags for one photo," she continued, the words natural and instinctive.

I had the urge to cut her off right then and there, making her delete all her accounts and vow to never again share her thoughts online. Though when Cole shot me a smile, I couldn't help but laugh. Whether we wanted to believe it or not, she was speaking our language. At some point between her first tweet and hundredth selfie, she stopped being just our mom and started becoming a friend (and a guaranteed like on every photo and status we posted).

Her new knowledge of social media and things like trending topics and viral videos also allowed her to understand my career a lot better. Before her journey into the virtual world, she, like so many baby boomers, had a difficult time understanding how I was supporting myself by doing "Internet things." Most of her friends and older clients assumed my job as the managing editor of a website was just a hobby, and would inquire about what I actually did for money. Before she understood it herself, her answers would sound like cop-outs, but now she had the ability to give it to them straight. She'd brag about my being verified on Twitter and tell everyone that I basically had full control over what people read online. Of course, mothers are naturals at making their kids' responsibilities sound slightly grander than they actually are.

Mothers are also naturals at embarrassing their kids, regardless of how many likes they rack up on Instagram. My mom, in particular, would post at least one naked baby picture of me a month. That might be fine, but for reasons I'll never understand, a handful of my business acquaintances and friends had begun to follow her. It's nice to know the guy who interviewed me for a podcast the night before, asking me just hours earlier about being a young professional in digital media, got to wake up to my butt crack on his newsfeed the next morning.

The day she hashtagged "lumbersexual" under a picture of my dad standing outside, I considered not going home for Christmas. If you're unaware, *lumbersexual* is the term used to describe attractive, rugged men who do things like wear flannel and tackle bears in their spare time. In the picture, my father, the fifty-eight-year-old nurse manager, was wearing the only flannel shirt he owned.

Absurdity became part of my mother's online brand, though of course she had no clue what a brand even was or that she had one. My mom's being so active online was as unexpected as it was entertaining for the people who knew her best—mainly because she was truly good at it. She possessed the same lack of self-consciousness that allows children to learn languages so quickly, and people loved it. Soon, she'd become synonymous with social media in my family and throughout her circle of friends.

One of my good friends, a well-known New York City fashion designer, texted me one night asking if Marie Dybec was actually my mother.

"Yup, that's her," I replied.

"We're each other's Instagram fans," she wrote back. "Very modern mama."

This was coming from a woman who's been featured on the *Forbes* "30 Under 30" list, and whose job it is to reinvent the concept of modern and turn it into something people can wear. It was the first time I feared my own mother might understand the whole social-media game better than I did.

I decided to call my very modern mama one night after she posted a picture of her new white leather Chuck Taylors and a long cape-like shirt she purchased after I said it looked like something Kanye West would wear. I felt compelled to tell her how cool she was, and I really meant it.

She laughed it off. "Trust me, I'm really not trying to be cool. Though, I have to say, it is difficult to find other people my age that really get social media."

"So how are you so good at it?" I asked.

"I don't think I'm good," she replied. "To be honest, the only reason I got into it was to connect with you more."

It was only a few months earlier that she had called me, doing her best to fight back tears, and explained that building my own life was important, but pointless if I pushed family aside. Admittedly, I'd gone through the first couple of years living on my own using the excuse "sorry, I'm just too busy" more times than the term "broken record" could ever apply to. It was shortly after that conversation that I pulled my head out of my ass and that she showed an interest in social media. I like to think she woke up one morning and thought, "Well, if my son's gone missing I may as well look for him on the Internet. That's where his kind spend most of their time anyway."

"You know, I miss the days when you were oblivious and needed my help," I told her. "It feels like just yesterday you had trouble turning your computer on. Now you're completely independent. I think I'm experiencing empty-nest syndrome."

"Don't worry," she laughed, "I'll never really understand any of this. No matter how much it seems like I get it."

I was home visiting for Christmas a few weeks later when she pulled me aside like she had a burdening secret to get off her chest.

"This social-media thing is starting to scare me," she admitted.

She told me that she had just learned that morning that an old friend had separated from her husband a few months back. It wasn't so much the tarnished wedding vows that disturbed her, but more so the fact that she never would have known based on this person's seemingly happy and frequently updated Facebook page.

For the first time, social media wasn't the fun, relationship-building activity it had always been for her. It had become something far more complex. Something as capable of dishonesty and deceit as any person walking the streets. In that moment, as she stood in front of me disappointed and confused, moments away from a wave of family members walking through our front door chock-full of Christmas cheer, I felt for her. I had experienced this sort of Internet fallout countless times, and it can take you by surprise.

"You know," she finally said, "this reminds me of when I was younger and would drive around rich neighborhoods during the holidays. The houses were always so beautifully decorated and I just assumed that the families inside were having a better Christmas than everyone else."

In my mind I imagined a quiet suburban street lined with robust, two-story homes, decorated from top to bottom in lights as white as snow and wreaths the size of truck tires. I pictured thick smoke rising from the tops of chimneys and shiny, plastic reindeer grazing motionless on front lawns next to winding driveways overflowing with European sports cars. But behind the elaborate display worth at least a thousand Instagram likes, there was nothing. No laughter-filled dinners and borderline food fights. No watching the same Christmas movie for the thousandth time because it was tradition. No gifts under the tree that were purchased with any true consideration. And certainly no mothers who had become hashtag sluts for the sake of their children.

The Uber Diaries

I recently had a conversation with an Uber driver that went something like this:

> DRIVER. You are very good at Uber.
>
> ME. What do you mean? You're the driver, not me.
>
> DRIVER. You have five-star rating. You are VIP customer.
>
> ME. That's amazing. What does that mean exactly?
>
> DRIVER. Every driver rated you five out of five. You are the perfect customer. You give no problems.
>
> ME. That's great. I've never had a bad experience with Uber. I use it all the time. In fact, I may be addicted to it.
>
> DRIVER. It's a pleasure to drive you, sir.

I looked down at the open Uber app on my phone, which told me my driver's name was Vural and that he had a rating of 4.8 stars out of five. As far as I knew, there was no way to view your rating as a customer, so it was the first time I was hearing about my apparently flawless record. The conversation went on in similar fashion for the remainder of the ride. Vural couldn't seem to get over the fact he was speaking with a five-star customer. I felt like a unicorn in his backseat, and he treated me as such.

Vural explained how he had journeyed from Turkey to New York City more than twenty years ago, and that driving for Uber allowed him to finally be his own boss. He had two small daughters and a wife at home. Before he was an Uber driver he was struggling as a taxi driver and, as he put it, doing some things he wasn't so proud of. I didn't push for details.

"I have some bad customers, some good customers," he said. "But you, my friend, are the very best. I will rate you five stars and keep you perfect."

This remark was strange for a couple of reasons. Firstly, my perfect rating was in the hands of a complete stranger. What if he'd been having a bad day and only rated me four stars? What if he was like one of those college professors who doesn't believe in perfect and abides by the "A+ is a myth" mentality? Secondly, it was hard to imagine I was providing the most intriguing and cordial conversation he'd ever had with a customer. Was I only the best because I had a five-star rating already? He didn't really get to know me before determining I was the best. If I hadn't entered his car with a five-star rating, would Vural even like me?

I tried to think back to all my previous Uber rides—there have been many, too many—and couldn't think of a time I hadn't given a driver five stars. It was the same routine each time. They'd pick me up, drop me at my destination, and when the ride was over I'd quickly slide my finger to the right, highlighting all the rating stars that appeared on my phone's screen. Apparently my drivers had been doing the same.

While I'd never overthought the rating system, Uber itself had become an undeniable part of my life, falling somewhere between water and shelter on my priority list. The first time I used the touch-of-a-button car service I was stuck in the rain after a late night at the office. Every taxi that passed by was occupied. A friend from work had told me to download the Uber app earlier in the day but I never did. So under the cover of a deli awning I downloaded the app, entered my credit-card information, and requested a car. Within minutes, a brand new Honda Accord pulled up right in front of me. I looked over at a couple searching hopelessly for a cab across the street and climbed in, unsure whether or not I was going to be chopped up in tiny pieces and sold on the black market or delivered safely to my apartment.

Luckily, the latter happened, and since that first time I've become increasingly dependent on the ability to pull out my phone and have a car show up within minutes. This service is especially useful in New York City, where I don't own a car and try to avoid the crowded subways at all costs, even if it means cringing over credit statements reminding me of my expensive new habit. I was most likely hooked on Uber so quickly because

I am both a sucker for convenience and even more of a sucker for any opportunity to feel luxurious. This absolutely includes having a black Escalade pick me up, even if I'm just going a few blocks down the street or back to my apartment alone.

As I stepped out of Vural's car in front of my apartment, he once again noted that he'd give me a five-star rating. I assured him I'd be doing the same and we shared our final good-byes. Once I was settled in my apartment I opened the Uber app and waited for the rating screen to pop up so I could give Vural his five stars and move on. Except the rating screen never appeared. I checked my inbox for the Uber receipt, which includes a link to the rating option, though the e-mail was nowhere to be found. I set my phone aside and figured the e-mail would come through eventually. As I continued on with my night, heating up food and washing some dishes, I couldn't help but check my phone every two minutes. Then I was struck with the thought of Vural waiting anxiously for me to submit my rating. I imagined him checking his phone every few minutes as well, slowly losing all hope he had in humanity as he considered the possibility that a five-star customer wasn't true to his word. If Vural went back to doing things he wasn't proud of, the burden would be on me.

Even more concerning to me was the possibility Vural would reciprocate what he perceived as a slight by giving me a low rating. I wondered if most drivers waited for their ratings to come in before rating their customers, if that's how the process even worked. I was suddenly enraged by the fact that my perfect rating, which I'd only found out about that night, could be tarnished due to a technical glitch. So I did something I'd never done before. I called an Uber driver after I'd already been dropped off.

Uber lists both the driver and passenger's phone numbers within the app, though the contact information is only available during the duration of a ride. Luckily I'd called Vural before he'd picked me up to explain in detail which street corner I was standing on, so I still had his number in my phone. After two rings Vural picked up, his voice an excited chirp on the other end of the line.

"Mr. Perfect!" he exclaimed. "How are you?"

"Listen, Vural," I frantically explained. "The Uber app never gave me the option to rate you. And I never got the receipt e-mailed, so I can't rate you that way either."

There was brief silence before Vural responded. "My friend," he started, "you do not need to worry about a thing. Uber is very busy right now. You will get the e-mail in time." His voice was calm and reassuring, like a grandparent you love or doctor you trust.

"You will be happy to know," he continued, "I have already rated you five stars. You are perfect still."

I thanked Vural and wished him a good night, which in reality meant a good life. The call ended and I felt a warm comfort consume me.

"Mr. Perfect," I mumbled to myself, laughing.

If I'm being honest with myself, Vural telling me I had a five-star rating changed Uber for me forever. Before my encounter with Vural, Uber rides were peaceful. Even if I did use the service to feel like someone important with a personal driver, Uber rides were still a place where I was able to gather my thoughts and breathe after hectic workdays or relax on the way to a restaurant or event. After all, I was paying for that luxury of solitude and convenience you can't find on the subway during rush hour. Knowing I had a five-star rating to protect transformed me into a different kind of passenger. A passenger desperate to impress and dazzle, not sit back and relax. Each Uber ride after Vural's may as well have been a first date or audition for *The Real World*. In the back of every Uber, I was part myself and part whoever it was I thought the stranger in the front seat wanted me to be. If the driver had on a Yankees hat I'd complain about the previous night's pitching or talk about how much I missed Jeter. If they had a picture of their kids on the dashboard I'd pretend like I was thinking about becoming a father. It wasn't dishonesty as much as it was being a good conversationalist. This led to more intimate conversations with strangers than I expected.

I began keeping notes on particular rides once I realized just how open some of the drivers were willing to be once they knew I was interested in hearing what they had to say. I also assume Uber customers are generally split between two demographics: the ones who say hello then sit quietly on their phones, and the drunk customers, who sync their shitty playlists with the car radio, talk about vulgar sexual experiences with their friends, and ask the driver to stop at McDonald's for late-night Big Macs and milkshakes. A lot of these drunken customers probably throw up in the back of the car, too. I only did this once, but luckily someone else had ordered the Uber, so my rating wasn't affected after blowing chunks out the window, but really all over the outside of the car. Some of the most memorable conversations with my drivers are the following, which have been partly transcribed to best reflect the original dialogue.

The Cheating Husband

It's safe to say I may be the only person in New York City, or perhaps the world, who has witnessed their Uber driver cry. It wasn't a heavy flowing cry with sobs and dripping snot, but there were tears and one definitive sniffle.

The ride started out normal. I got picked up on a Wednesday night from the same spot I get picked up every Wednesday night after playing basketball with a bunch of guys from Elite Daily. My driver was particularly quiet, and it worried me that sitting silent in the backseat could lead to an average rating, like four stars. Not a bad rating, but not perfect. You never know exactly what a driver's rubric is.

I broke the silence by asking him how his night was going. He took his time to find the words, and then responded, "The night gives you too much time to think." Just like that it was the darkest, most personal Uber ride I'd ever been on. Not to mention, he delivered the line with such conviction and honesty that if I remember correctly, I felt the hair on my arms stand up.

Imagine Dylan Thomas driving you around New York City while reciting,

Do not go gentle into that good night,
Old age should burn and rave close of day;
Rage, rage against the dying of the light.

I'm not one of those people who are good at memorizing quotes. I wish I were. I respect the people who can, at the drop of a hat, recall a sentence so perfectly architected and considered by someone historical and great and use it in everyday conversation. Though, there is one Van Gogh quote that I'd always remembered but never used. Finally, my time had come.

I swallowed, and with a shaky, completely unconfident voice, squeaked out the words, "'I often think that the night is more alive and richly colored than the day.' Vincent Van Gogh said that. You know, the painter."

The driver remained silent, possibly considering the message, possibly ignoring me altogether. After successfully merging onto the entrance to the Queensboro Bridge, he spoke up.

DRIVER. Tonight is the night I will tell my wife I have failed her.

ME. [*after taking at least ten seconds to process what I'd heard*] What happened?

DRIVER. [*after taking at least ten seconds to carefully search for the answer to my question*] I will tell my wife of twenty-one years that I have been unfaithful.

[*Okay, just assume there was at least a ten-second delay between each response.*]

ME. Maybe she will understand.

DRIVER. She will understand what is true. That I am no longer the man she married.

ME. You're strong for telling her.

DRIVER. I am the weakest I've ever been.

Through the silent pauses I could hear his muffled sobs. I decided to give the conversation a rest and let him be. As we moved slowly over the unusually crowded bridge, the Manhattan skyline stood tall and shimmering off to our right, a home to so many secrets.

The Conspiracy Theorist

After getting picked up at the airport I noticed the book *Behold a Pale White Horse* on my driver's dashboard. The book is basically any conspiracy theorist's bible, written by Milton William Cooper, an alleged ex-military man who claimed he had evidence of a number of government cover-ups, from HIV and AIDS being a man-made illness to the truth about extraterrestrials. More specifically, he claimed John F. Kennedy was assassinated because he was about to tell America that aliens were taking over the world. Cooper was killed in 2001 after shooting a police officer in the head. Ever since his book's release, he had claimed the government was after him.

I asked my driver how he liked the book, telling him I'd always been interested in checking it out. He turned toward me with a look of anguish, his face like a balloon fighting the urge to pop, his foot still pressing down on the gas pedal.

"Can I tell you something?" he asked. "Like really tell you something?"

"Sure," I replied.

The bulk of the conversation went something like this:

DRIVER. Do you know much about this stuff? You know, the Illuminati, government cover-ups? That kind of stuff.

ME. I've heard things.

DRIVER. I've been probing deep, man. Too deep I think. Last week I heard this weird noise on the phone while I was talking to a friend. I googled the sound afterward and it fit the description of a wiretap.

ME. Who do you think would be listening in on your calls?

DRIVER. Who do you think? The government. The American government. The Mexican government. It doesn't matter, man.

They're all connected anyway. You know, they're all working to form one universal government with one currency. That's what I was telling my friend about on the phone.

ME. Like the New World Order conspiracy?

DRIVER. If you want to call it a conspiracy. Look, I know there are some crazy people out there, but I only focus on facts. You know there's fluoride in the water we drink, right? That's a fact.

ME. I guess so.

DRIVER. Well there is. There's fluoride in the water we drink, and do you know what fluoride does to us?

ME. I'm not exactly sure.

DRIVER. It's like poison to a specific part of our brain. The pineal gland, which is the part of our brain that allows us to connect with spiritual dimensions and think at a higher level. It's our third eye. The right dose of daily fluoride actually shrinks the gland and calcifies it, and when it shrinks, we become more submissive and don't question things. We just do what we're told. How do you explain that?

I'd witnessed firsthand the effects that diving too deep into conspiracy theories can have on a person. An old roommate of mine had also read *Behold a Pale White Horse* and watched every conspiracy video on YouTube known to man. It got to a point in which I couldn't even watch television without his pointing out every triangle that represented the Illuminati and demonic symbol that an untrained eye wouldn't notice. Once he physically had to leave the room because of how satanically charged an AT&T commercial was.

Granted, a lot has gone unanswered in this swelling, sinister world of ours. A lot of government cover-ups and global scandals have been uncovered. But it seems to slightly defeat the purpose of a valid conspiracy when someone believes in all the possibilities. Is it the aliens or the freemasons pulling the strings? The Illuminati or the devil? Are they all at a round table somewhere hoarding Cuban cigars and face-timing Beyoncé?

If it were a normal, casual conversation I were having, I'd happily play devil's advocate and mention that there are potential benefits to fluoride in water and that global governance seems highly unlikely. Though, this wasn't a normal conversation. This was an Uber ride, and I couldn't risk damaging my five-star rating because the driver sensed my doubt that the world was one big rotating lie in an unexplored universe. So instead of questioning his rationale, I nodded in agreement.

"It makes a lot of sense when you put it that way," I told him.

He spent the remainder of the ride rattling off videos for me to watch and articles to read. We idled in front of my apartment for about ten minutes so he could finish explaining the reptilian theory, which is the belief that the world is actually controlled by shape-shifting reptiles that took the form of humans and gained full political power.

"That last theory is a little out there," he admitted. "But you just never know. You really just never know."

The Slow Driver

The only time I ever considered not rating a driver five stars was one morning when I had an early flight to catch. The Uber picked me up at my apartment and I expressed I was running a bit behind schedule and needed to hurry to the airport. I should have jumped out of the Uber and called another one the moment my driver began talking about the newly enforced speed limits in New York City, which required twenty-five miles per hour on any normal roads and forty miles per hour on highways. Of course, I respect the laws and especially any rules that facilitate personal safety, but the fact of the matter is nobody actually drives forty miles per hour on a highway. In fact, it seems unsafe to drive at such low speeds while everyone around you is going at least double the speed limit.

My driver, however, took the rules to heart. He didn't go a half mile per hour over twenty-five on side roads, and cruised at exactly forty miles per hour on the parkway. I watched help-lessly out the window as old ladies in Buicks whizzed by and '92 Saturns looked like they were being driven by Dale Earnhardt Jr. Worst of all, his GPS took him off the parkway and onto Queens Boulevard, which is not a highway and therefore required a strict twenty-five-mile-per-hour speed limit.

What was even worse was the pressure that was building up in my bladder as the driver crept at a snail's pace toward the air-port. I knew I should have gone to the bathroom before I left my apartment, but I also didn't know the most law-abiding person in America would be my driver. There wasn't even traffic on the road.

The attempt to keep my frustration to myself wasn't easy. On one hand, my driver was literally the only person following the speed limit. On the other hand, if I spoke up there was a chance of getting into a contentious conversation that could have an impact on my rating. In most circumstances, having a full bladder with no outlet to empty it takes precedence over almost everything else. I couldn't hold back.

ME. Please, sir, do you think you could go a little faster? You will not be pulled over for going ten miles per hour faster than the speed limit, especially since everyone around us is going at least seventy.

DRIVER. No, the police are strict now about the new rule. Drivers must follow the rules.

ME. Yes, but wouldn't everyone be pulled over if they were that strict? Like all the cars that are passing us right now?

DRIVER. This job is all I have, sir. If I lose this job I have nothing, you understand? One ticket and I will lose my taxi license and make no money. I have a family. What do I tell my family if I lose my job? Will you take care of them?

ME. I understand, but I have to go to the bathroom really bad. Like this makes the cut for top ten moments I've had to pee really, really badly.

DRIVER. So your pee is more important than my family?

I sat silently in the backseat, mystified by how the conversation had so quickly arrived at a point in which the value of my urine was being compared to a man's family. I decided not to push the issue any further. Was a battle with a driver who ultimately had full control over how hard he pressed on the gas pedal really worth a lower Uber rating? As difficult as it was to remain quiet in the backseat of a car that may as well have been a parade float, with a bladder on the verge of bursting, I made the call to preserve my premier customer status. As a New Yorker, I felt weak and ashamed. But as a loyal Uber customer, I felt smart. *This is what you sometimes have to do to get ahead*, I thought to myself. There's a reason not everyone has a five-star rating.

"No, my pee is not more important than your family," I added before closing my eyes and doing my best to hold it in.

The Voice of Reason

Despite the, at times, tiresome effort to be talkative and polite during Uber rides since Vural told me about my five-star rating, it was rewarding to know I was successfully earning my rank as a perfect customer. I even considered reaching out to Uber to ask the percentage of frequent users around the world who actually maintained a five-star rating. Maybe I'd even get some complimentary rides out of it. On top of remaining perfect, I'd had some memorable and entertaining conversations with strangers, just by listening to what they had to say. At some point, being an enthusiastic/conversational/caring/cordial customer became second nature. It was like a hobby only I knew about. More like a second job.

One night I got the idea to simply ask my Uber driver what my rating was. It was during a quick ride from my office to a work event uptown. I was talking to my driver about how he liked Uber and what he thought about its business strategy and technology. When we started talking about the rating system, I saw my opportunity and quickly asked if he could tell me what my rating was, partly so I could hear another driver boast about my five stars. It had been a while since the first time and I was seeking validation.

"You have a very high rating," he said. "You're a very good customer."

"I'm very proud of my five stars," I told him. "And I really respect what Uber drivers do."

"Five stars is very hard to get," he responded. "You have a rating of 4.8 out of 5. Very good rating. I don't see too many customers with a 4.8 rating. When I see them on the Uber app, I'm always happy."

I'd stopped listening once I heard the words *four point eight* come out of his mouth.

"Are you sure I don't have a five-star rating?" I asked.

"Friend, 4.8 is a very good rating," he replied.

The world froze for a few seconds in the back of that Uber as I filed through a mental Rolodex of potential suspects who could have given me a rating less than five stars. Was it the man who'd cheated on his wife? Had I probed too deeply into his personal matters? Did he decide to take his frustrations out on me? Could the conspiracy theorist sense my doubt? Did I argue one second too long with the frustratingly slow driver? Maybe it was a driver I didn't expect at all. Someone I'd complimented and gave my utmost attention.

"This is unbelievable," I mumbled out loud. I waited for my driver to console me but he didn't.

"I had a five-star rating a few months ago," I admitted. "I'm pretty upset to hear it went down. I never gave a driver any problem and I rated every single driver five stars."

The driver, like so many of the others, thought before he spoke, reaching in his mind for something honest and helpful, not only speaking for the sake of throwing out words and passing the time. It's a quality that's hard to come by, but surprisingly common among people who spend hours driving people around each day.

"You know, I have to say," he said, before trailing off into silence again. "You know, I want to change my answer from before. There is one problem with Uber and it's technology. It lets men decide the value of other men. That is too much power."

The driver was right. The ability to rate the value of another person is a lot of power and responsibility. In my notes about my Uber rides, which had become a strange diary of sorts, I scribbled down my conversation with him under the headline

"The Voice of Reason." Sure, I understand the rating system as a necessary component of a business that trusts people with the safety of others. Though some things are simply better left unknown. If there were a universal rating system in life, which determined our socioeconomic status or whether or not we'd experience a peaceful afterlife, and we were all aware of our ratings, the world wouldn't have many genuine people left. We'd all be living for the sake of pleasing whoever was judging us— hearing but not really listening; talking but not actually saying anything; going from point a to point b without ever considering the journey in between.

Breakup, Breakdown

My first real relationship was in seventh grade. At the time I'd only kissed a handful of girls, though one make-out session in middle school is equivalent to about three one-night stands as an adult. The girl I was dating was named Nicole. She was a cute cheerleader with blonde hair and a nice house. Nicer than most of the kids' houses at my school. I asked her to be my girlfriend the same night a copycat version of the Harlem Globetrotters performed at my school. One of the players threw me his sweat-stained purple headband after the game and I gave it to Nicole as a symbol of my commitment. From that point on she carried it everywhere she went.

Our relationship was strong for about three weeks, and then Valentine's Day came. I woke up the morning of Valentine's Day twenty minutes before my bus came with no gift for Nicole. Desperate, I dug through my closet in hopes of finding something red or heart shaped. The only possible gift option I came across was a Sylvester the Cat stuffed animal I'd won at a carnival months earlier. It had been sitting all that time under the weight of sneakers and sports equipment and its body had become wrinkled and half collapsed. It looked like a homeless Sylvester with severe facial palsy. I had no choice but to stuff it into my backpack and head to the bus stop. At school I quickly threw it into my locker. Luckily Nicole was late to school and we'd have to exchange gifts at the end of the day.

Once classes were over I slowly made my way to my locker to meet Nicole. When I arrived she was waiting with flowers and a chocolate heart the size of her torso. I considered running in the other direction, but it was too late. There was no turning back. All I could do was pray that Sylvester was her favorite *Looney Tunes* character.

Unfortunately, Sylvester is nobody's favorite *Looney Tunes* character. If anything, he's arguably the most perverted and diabolical *Looney Tunes* character. When I pulled his limp, wrinkled body from the bottom of my locker, Nicole's face went from a smile to utter confusion in the time it takes Bugs Bunny to say, "That's all, folks." We walked out of school in silence before getting on our respective buses, me with chocolate and flowers, her with a secondhand carnival prize.

Later that day, I was outside playing basketball with a friend when my mom yelled to me from the house: "There's someone named Michelle on the phone for you." Michelle was Nicole's best friend. I picked up the phone and she gave it to me straight. She told me Nicole was embarrassed and hurt by my gift and that she didn't want to be my girlfriend anymore. It was over. Just like that my first relationship turned into my first breakup, and the news was delivered through a third party. The next day at school I asked Nicole for my sweat-stained purple headband back.

Nicole's breaking up with me was the first time I realized the fragile nature of relationships. Granted, on the day of the Big Break, I went right back outside and finished playing basketball, but it was the beginning of what would be a long streak of getting dumped. It took me a while to realize relationships took effort, and for some reason I always felt a step behind. They say girls mature faster than boys do, and I think it was true in my case.

My next girlfriend after Nicole was also a cheerleader. Her name was Lauren and she happened to be one of Nicole's close friends. She was the girl every guy in school had a crush on. I figured she'd heard about my poor gift-giving abilities from Nicole, so the fact she still gave me a chance made me like her even more. Lauren was the first girl I felt any real sexual attraction toward. We didn't actually have sex, but I'd sneak off with her any chance I got for intimate make-out sessions in strange places, mostly the public library. We'd have our parents drop us off separately, claiming we had group projects we had to work on. Then we'd run off to the most hidden corner of the library and kiss passionately against a wall of books. Looking back, it was an intense affair for a couple of seventh graders.

What went wrong with Lauren was that while she was ready to take our relationship to the next level and do things like go to the mall together and hold hands, I was fixated on making out in the library. It was all I could think about. My daily thoughts were consumed by the desire to make out with Lauren against a wall of old books, despite the fact we'd done it countless times. Eventually she got tired of the same routine and called it quits. That's when I learned that a key factor of being in a relationship is exploring new things, no matter how good of a kisser you think you are. Lauren grew up to become a professional cheerleader for an NFL team, so I still get to see her on Sundays a few times a year. Oddly enough, I do get the urge to visit a library when her face pops up on my TV.

After middle school came high school, and that's when relationships became trickier and breakups got ugly. Before high school, breakups were just small bumps in the road that were easy to shrug off. If Nicole didn't like my terrible gifts I'd find a girl that did. If Lauren was tired of making out in the library then I'd date a girl who'd never made out in a library before. Getting over people was simple and didn't come with any prolonged mental abuse. High school is usually, for most people, when breaking up makes you realize you've got a lot more emotion inside of you than you'd thought. Mostly anger and jealousy.

The first time I learned that a relationship could be truly toxic was in tenth grade when I started dating a girl named

Andrea from a few towns over. She was exotic and sexy and was the first girl to cheat on me. The phone call I made to her the day I found out she cheated was the first time in my life I felt I'd acted purely off instinct. The moment she picked up the phone I was overtaken by a rage I didn't know I had. I yelled and cried and reprimanded her for not honoring the agreement to be my exclusive girlfriend. I felt wronged and needed to make it clear how hurt I was. Most of all I felt like a stranger had taken and used something that was mine and only mine. For some reason I kept using the analogy, "If someone broke into my house and started playing my PlayStation I'd be furious."

After all the yelling and crying I decided to give the relationship another try. I thought I was being generous, but looking back, I was afraid of change. It was easier to be miserable with someone who had hurt me than go through the process of finding someone new. I'm not sure why we ever do this, but I especially don't understand why we do it when we're young and have the most energy we'll ever have in our lives. Maybe we like being in relationships in which we feel the person who wronged us owes us something. We think we'll forever have a "get out of jail free" card because they were the ones who fucked up first. This, of course, is never the case.

As soon as I hung up with Andrea I remember thinking, "What just took over my body and made me say the things I said and feel the things I'm feeling?" I'd never felt so strongly about anything in my life. It took everything in me not to call her back and repeat everything I'd just said just to be sure she understood how shitty she made me feel.

This is how relationships and breakups go for a while when we're young enough to be naive about most things but old enough to make sex a priority. We view the people we're interested in as the most physical versions of themselves that we can show off like new shoes. We don't really consider their personality, sense of humor, or quirks. We mostly just consider how labeling them our boyfriend or girlfriend will make us look. The inevitable outcome of most of these relationships (except for the high-school sweethearts who somehow find a way to make it work) is savage breakups and bloodthirsty arguments. After all, we don't really know the people we've decided to date at that age. We just know how they look and dress and where they fall on the spectrum of high-school popularity. So when they do act in a way we didn't expect or show a side we couldn't have guessed existed, we're shocked and angry and demand explanations.

It's a messy period, but it's also an essential one. At least I like to think so. Sure, most high-school breakups stem from cheating, or jealousy, or a general overly possessive nature, but at least during those breakups we're learning to identify some qualities we don't like. Sometimes we fight to prove our innocence: "She only called me because she had a question about the homework." Sometimes we fight to dismantle someone else's innocence: "I know for a fact you were talking to Jake at lunch yesterday." At the very least, we're learning to stand up for what we believe in.

That's an important lesson, even if you're an awkward teenager yelling into the phone loud enough to express anger but quiet enough so your parents don't hear from upstairs.

Though more than anything, the messy period of arguments and grade-school drama helps prepare us for a whole new and unexpected stage of relationships: college relationships. And with college relationships come college breakups.

College relationships are great because we finally start dating people for their personalities and points of view. They are also terrible because in college people's personalities and points of view change with the wind. In turn, the breakups consist of fewer raging indictments and more selfish laments. *This person doesn't understand my poetry. They don't respect my need for freedom. They don't watch foreign films. How could I be with a person that's not helping my soul evolve? They're holding me back.* If high-school breakups are about understanding what you don't like about other people, then college breakups are about finding what you do like about yourself. Or at least we think that's what they're about at the time. In college, the entire world is in front of you. Any and every dream is still fresh and possible. All you know is personal growth and freedom, not personal finances and corporate structure. Relationships aren't built to sustain college.

Personally, I was a sucker for this stage of breakups. I may have even started craving them. I couldn't help but feel each new breakup further fueled my creativity. I figured every aspiring writer thrived on pain, isolation, and the validation that people don't *get* you. I loved the person I was during those breakups. I was capable of Academy Award–worthy monologues at the drop of a hat. I'd use obscure movie references to describe how I was feeling and quote Nietzsche in my "good-bye forever I hope you find happiness in life" Facebook messages. Music had so much more purpose after these breakups. I'd listen to Radiohead and Bon Iver under the stars and feel like the most important misunderstood person in the universe. It was terribly narcissistic, but I have no doubt each one of those overly dramatic, perversely self-centered breakups helped me discover something new about myself. And isn't college really just about discovering yourself?

I once broke up with a girl in college because I needed a good personal narrative for a creative-writing class I was taking. I had writer's block for weeks and finally decided I'd write about what it's like to break up with someone simply for the sake of writing about it. In my mind it was some great artistic exploration. My professor's notes were that it was extreme and mean. The girl didn't take it well either, but I told her I was using artistic license. I was *that* guy.

Luckily, I was able to stop being that guy once I started getting into a few more serious relationships. The type of relationships that don't end a few weeks after they begin. I even got into one relationship that lasted beyond college and revolved around that scary four-letter *l* word that's not lust. Breakups become an entirely different monster once relationships are established on the foundation of love. To fall in love is to say, "I trust you enough that you won't hurt me." It's a confirmation with yourself that after years of mistakes and personal discovery, you have finally determined what makes someone ideal in your eyes. When these relationships don't go as planned, it's difficult to admit you were wrong. Nobody likes admitting they wasted time with something they thought was a sure thing. In turn, breakups tend to avoid the real issues altogether, and instead focus on problems that are irrelevant in the grand scheme of things. For some reason it's easier to blame a failed relationship on the way your partner chews their food than to look them in the eyes and admit, "I'm just not in love with you anymore." It's less of a struggle to tell someone they spend too much time thinking about their career than to just say you feel you're too young to settle down.

One of my most ridiculous breakups came in the middle of what ended up being an on-and-off four-year relationship with a girl named Amber. We'd been fighting for months and the relationship was on a steep and obvious decline. We'd gotten lazy and comfortable and sought more than we could provide for each other. She was more interested in planning a stable life together and I was ready to leave the suburbs as quickly as I could to pursue a writing career in New York City. Even the sex, when it happened, was nothing more than muscle memory. We were both so afraid of throwing away four years of effort that we kept pulling apart then coming back together, like a rubber band begging to just snap.

One day we were sitting in her room when she told me, with conviction, that she could beat me in a race. I'm not sure where the idea came from, but I immediately jumped up, furious, and demanded that she put on sneakers and meet me outside. Then she told me she thought it would be a close game if she played me in basketball one on one. This assertion pushed me over the edge. If there's one thing I take too seriously in life, it's basketball. I still have hoop dreams, despite the fact I'm five foot nine and the last time I played on an organized team was middle school. I still hold onto hope that a European scout will see me playing in the park and offer me a contract to be the star of some obscure team in Estonia or Latvia. If the opportunity ever came, I'd drop everything I'm doing and devote my life to ball in a heartbeat. So when Amber, who had never played a game of competitive basketball in her life, looked at me with a straight face and said it'd be a close game, I couldn't handle it. I told her it'd be an embarrassment and that she wouldn't even score a point if we played to one thousand. We eventually decided it'd be better if we spent some time apart and I left her house.

We ended up getting back together, and then broke up again shortly after because she said my healthy eating habits were annoying and she needed to be with someone who could eat cake and pizza whenever she wanted. The on-again-off-again cycle continued for about another year. Neither of us wanted to be the one to throw in the towel and call it quits. Eventually we just started seeing other people, which pretty much confirmed things were over.

During a breakup you spend so much time defending who you are and why you're that way that you end up getting to know yourself better than you ever have. There's a certain beauty in breakups for this reason. I spend too much time on a daily basis focused on my insecurities and worrying what people are going to think of me, so when I'm suddenly sticking up for myself, it's like a refreshing glass of water that makes me realize how thirsty I'd been all along.

Maybe all the breakups in our lives are just reminders there's still a lot we have to learn about ourselves before relying on other people for happiness. If anything, breakups should be renamed breakdowns. That's all they really are. Whatever drew two people together in the first place eventually breaks down, and then, more often than not, *we* end up breaking down as a result. But when that breakdown is over, and we get up off the floor with wounds that have finally healed, it's amazing how capable we are of building ourselves up again. It's strange to admit, but some of my most defining moments and clear-minded decisions have come right after breakups, when I was prepared to be selfish and focus on my own well-being.

Maybe the real definition of love is finding someone who doesn't cause you to break down in order to build yourself up. Someone who gives you the support you need to build yourself up each day, little by little. Someone who just wants to make out in the library once in a while, or who doesn't think about whether or not they could beat you in a race or score on you in basketball.

The New American Dream

The American Dream has faked his own death and reemerged as something far more contemporary and sociable. He ditched his gray flannel suit for running shoes and a man bun. He sold his two-story home with a white picket fence for a small room in an industrial warehouse turned communal-living space in Brooklyn. The building is occupied mostly by website developers, a few actors who have gotten steady extra work since graduating from their respective conservatories, and a grocery store cashier who once uploaded a YouTube video that has since amassed 327,543 views.

The American Dream is no longer a follower of established commercialism. And certainly no longer in pursuit of a steady paycheck. The American Dream is entrepreneurial and driven by the kind of ideas that make people irate because they didn't think of them first. The people who achieve this new American Dream are more than dreamers. They challenge the norm and disrupt the existing condition. They don't consider social mobility to have limits or rules. They are out there, conjuring up million-dollar ideas on their laptops, in their pajamas. Perhaps right this second. Every great brand was a startup at some point. Every great idea almost thrown out and abandoned because of a shred of doubt.

I've put together a short list of ideas I believe have great potential to succeed. Consider it my gift to you, the reader. They are at least worth the price of this book. What the world needs is ideas that are even less unafraid and unashamed than the success stories we currently look up to. If the future is now, then what comes next? It's up to us to decide. There are plenty of brilliant ideas out there, yet to be discovered and harnessed. So with these ideas as starters, grab your laptop, go to a coffee shop full of failed screenwriters, and give birth to the future of the future.*

Trendy's Supermarket

Whole Foods is a Fortune 500 company. It's publicly traded. It generates annual revenue in the tens of billions. It's also the devil's playground and everyone knows it. Yet we still shop

....

* If anyone actually wants to pursue one of these ideas I will give you Mark Cuban's e-mail address and connect you with other real investors. Just keep in mind I own a 20 percent stake in the business. This is nonnegotiable.

there. And it makes us feel good. It makes us feel modern and connected with a world we don't quite understand. A world in which asparagus water is sold for six dollars a bottle. A world in which camel milk is on the rise and kale has made its way into our ice cream.

Well if people want ridiculously expensive, insane sounding food items, then they deserve to have just that. And the truth is, Whole Foods isn't going to cut it anymore. I'm convinced people protest Whole Foods because Whole Foods pretends to be something it's not. As an organization, Whole Foods acts like it's not a big deal that they charge ten dollars for things like egg-white chips and upwards of eighty bucks for organic honey.

This is where Trendy's Supermarket comes in. Trendy's will be the first unashamed, openly pretentious supermarket that takes the artisanal health craze to the next level. The beauty of Trendy's will be that it doesn't pretend to be something it's not. Trendy's slogan will be "You can't shop with us." Trendy employees will be required to wear flannel shirts around their waists. Where Whole Foods is enigmatic and untrustworthy, Trendy's will be transparent and honest. Yes, Trendy's overcharges. Yes, the food is so obscure it's probably doing your body no good. This is what people want. This is what they will spend their paychecks on. The proof is already out there, thanks to Trendy's less honest competitors, who will quickly be left in the dust.

Whole Foods can own the locally sourced vegetable and tofu ginger rice muffin market, because Trendy's will be offering food trends that don't even exist yet. Think locally sourced tap water in a bottle. What person in their right mind living in Montana wouldn't pay twenty dollars for a bottle of tap water from Anita's apartment in the Bronx? What trendsetting New York City dweller wouldn't want to sip on some abundantly refreshing H20 straight from the sink of Mark, a college professor living on the Oregon Coast? It's hard to imagine how overly priced the tap water from Alaska will be, but people will want it.

Of course, at Trendy's, all gluten-free products will have only ever been handled by gluten-free individuals. This includes the farmers, distributors, packagers, and Trendy's employees themselves. This way, customers know they are getting a true, fully gluten-free experience they can't get anywhere else. Trendy's also understands that anyone who still eats 7-grain bread also probably still uses an iPhone 5, so the store will serve nothing less than 143-grain products. All customers will also receive a free matcha latte, made with certified opossum milk and an all-natural sweetener made from the stomach lining of farm-raised, free-range house flies from Guatemala. Naturally, all produce will be picked by young Malaysian children whose sugar and carbohydrate intake will be monitored and whose skin tone can be considered "sun-kissed."

It's assumed that Trendy's top-selling products will be ornamental Mason jars filled with air from the Pamir Mountains in

Central Asia, specifically from a peak in Kyrgyzstan. It's time to give the people what they want.

Business lesson: Listen closely to the market, it will tell you exactly what people want more of.

rEalBOOK

Face it, the death of the book happened a long time ago. Paper books are antiquated devices that even I use as decorative trinkets in my apartment. There's nobody out there reading a book that isn't looking up between each paragraph to make sure everyone around them sees they are going through the effort to turn pages and protect their cover from creases. It's a respectable effort, but an unsustainable one.

From a business perspective, it's important to be ahead of the curve. We can all agree that one day we'll all be reading on tablets and probably even through retinal contacts so it looks like we're all just staring off into the distance. At least it's easier on your neck than staring down at your phone. That's progress.

But let's start with the idea that electronic reading devices and tablets will only become more advanced and widely used. Let's assume it's where the money is and the manufacturers of these products can act as publishers and offer authors deals worth way more than any traditional publisher ever could. So authors start writing e-books only. What happens to the paper book readers then?

What happens is rEalBook, the first of its kind paperback e-book concealer. Each rEalBook is designed to appear as a literary classic, with an original cover design and real pages that actually function. Except each page is cut out in the middle, the way movie characters use library books and Bibles to stash money and drugs. The cutout will be customized to securely fit any e-reading device. This way readers get the convenience of an e-book, but can hide the fact they are weak and conformed to the ease and popularity of modern technology, as long as they remember to turn a fake page every minute or so.

Business lesson: Nostalgia sells. Nostalgia always sells.

Rent-A-Baby

Have you ever sat by yourself or with a significant other on one of those tragically uneventful days and thought, I wish I had a dog right now? Of course you have. But maybe you live in a small apartment in a city and can't properly care for a dog. Or maybe you're shit poor, working two internships, and can barely feed yourself anything other than stale pasta and carefully designed artisanal lattes. You've probably thought to yourself, it would be great if I could have a dog for the day, or even a long weekend. Why can't we? Why can't we have a dog for a day? We can have a movie for a day without owning it. We can drive a car for a day without owning it. We can even, if you want to go down that road, have a sex partner for a day (or an hour) without ever having to see or speak to that person again. People pay for all of these temporary services, and people would sure as hell pay for a dog they don't have to bring to a veterinarian. There would also be no better first date than bringing a dog you don't own to the park.

Well, unfortunately this business already exists. I had the idea for a dog-renting business, which I'd call Rent-A-Paw, at least three years ago. But thanks to a new app called Bark'N'Borrow, you actually can borrow people's dogs.

Business lesson: If you have an idea you think is great, move on it immediately, because it's only a matter of time before someone else thinks of it.

Well, don't worry, there's still a great idea here. Let Bark'N'Borrow have their fun, we're thinking bigger now. So, back to square one. Have you ever been sitting by yourself or with your significant other and thought, I wish I could have practice taking care of a baby? Of course you have. But maybe you're just not ready to welcome a child into the world. Maybe you're unsure if you ever even want kids. You'd love to try without having to actually inseminate a woman or adopt. You're concerned about how you're going to pay their college tuition. Enter Rent-A-Baby, the first ever baby-borrowing business. Like Bark'N'Borrow, you could be a babysitter looking for work, or just someone who wants to spend a day with a baby.

I know what you're thinking: *How can we trust people to safely and responsibly watch a baby for the day?* When you're sitting at a round table with angel investors or dripping sweat on national television on *Shark Tank*, you look directly into the eyes of everyone in the room wearing a suit and tell them Rent-A-Baby will conduct top-of-the-line background checks on all interested customers. Of course, once they're in the system it will be easier to rent a new baby each time. Business is all about return customers. Rent-A-Baby will also provide an adequate amount of baby food and diapers (included in the rental fee). Renters will also be required to check in with Rent-A-Baby every hour using a live video feed or else they will be charged an additional fee.

A man with a suit more expensive than your parents' car and hair so thin and gray that you wonder why he doesn't just try the bald look may then raise his pen and ask you how Rent-A-Baby will operate if people don't want to let strangers take care of their babies. You look at that man, run your fingers through your thick head of young, vibrant hair and tell him Rent-A-Baby will work directly with local adoption agencies. The kicker is that when the renters are done with their babies, the immediate opportunity to adopt that baby is made readily available. And who wouldn't fall in love with a baby after spending a day with it? Suddenly your lucrative rental business is transformed into an organization that will lead to the nationwide increase in child adoption. That's when you find your face on the cover of *Time* magazine for its "100 Most Influential People" edition. You'll be saving the world and your bank account, one crying, snot-filled, perpetually hungry baby at a time.

Little Brother, Big Son

Reality TV is addictive. We all know it, even if we don't enjoy it. This idea is less of a strict business strategy and more of a creative entertainment pitch that will lead to instant stardom and unimaginable riches.

There is one requirement though. You must have a sibling. I'll use myself as an example since that's how the idea began. I have a younger brother, Cole. The initial idea was to figure out a way to gain legal custody of him. Then once that was established, we'd pitch a show to TLC called *Little Brother, Big Son*. Cameras would capture every unorthodox struggle and victory of having a younger brother who is also, legally, my twenty-one-year-old son. It would be an instant hit. There's not a soul in America who wouldn't tune in to that show on a weeknight after work.

Let's not even get started on the episode when Cole's ex-parents, now his grandparents, though still my parents, come to visit. Or better yet, the moment during season thirteen when Cole is married and has his first child, and in the same moment I become both a grandpa and an uncle.

The idea is yours for the taking.

Business lesson: Always be prepared to exploit yourself and others to achieve success.

Made of Money Interest Tracker

What parent hasn't uttered the phrase, "Does it look like I'm made of money?" The answer is none. It may, in fact, be one of the most commonly used phrases among parents, along with "I'm not going to ask you again" and "Are you deaf or something?"

There's no doubt that when it comes to finances, being a parent is strenuous and costly. Besides supporting yourself, kids are suddenly thrown into the equation. Little peanut-shaped bodies that don't know the value of a dollar, and, let's face it, may never understand it.

The amount of hard-earned money parents spend in a lifetime on their kids must be astronomical. And what do they get in return? They should be getting interest, for one. Their money does act as a loan after all. An investment, with the hopes their child-rearing and support throughout the years will result in a successful, money-making, sane member of society they can proudly call their kid. But that doesn't mean they don't deserve the proper return on their investment.

Made of Money Interest Tracker would be the perfect tool for parents. The service will electronically track all money that parents spend on their kids within the time period parents select. Each time they lend money to their child, pay their kid's rent, or buy them groceries, they can update the amount spent and Interest Tracker will automatically include the determined interest rate based on a percent mutually agreed upon by parents and child. Though, all a parent really needs to do is get a signature when the kid is eighteen, and that can be done early on a Saturday morning when they're tired and won't care to look at the fine print.

It would be pretty inhumane to track money spent on a child since birth, but Interest Tracker is perfect for parents whose millennial children are overstaying their welcome at home, refuse to get a job, or have been duped into paying a colossal New York City rent so their child can "find themselves" at a liberal arts school. After all, the average millennial income is somewhere around thirty thousand a year, and an increasing number of twenty-something-year-olds either never left their parents' home or are moving back in.

Some parents are nicer than others, and instead of asking for an eventual payment of the full amount of money spent plus interest, parents can select an option to simply request a small percentage back of total money spent. For example, maybe a parent just wants 3 percent back of the total amount of money they spent directly on their child from the child's twenty-first birthday up until whenever it is they can start paying their own phone bills and stop relying on Mom and Dad, who surely abandoned their retire-at-sixty plan a long time ago.

Many parents will wish Made of Money Interest Tracker were invented years ago. They would be expecting a pretty hefty return right about now. Though something tells me as millennials begin having babies and starting families, they'll be quick to jump on a service like this one. Especially because they know best just how much a kid can drain a family's life savings.

Business lesson: If you can find a way to save people money, you can make money.

Vintage Pal

There's been a steadily increasing interest in vintage clothing and accessories in America. I won't use the word hipster because I don't believe in it, but you catch my drift. Young people all over this great country flock to thrift stores to stock their wardrobe with used jeans and shirts from decades past. Sometimes you'll even find designer pieces among the musty sprawl.

Thrifting has become so popular that it's used as a verb. Personally, I have nothing against it. I've thrifted a handful of times in my life and have walked away with some great pieces of clothing I'd never have found otherwise. The only real problem with thrifting is that the search never really ends. You have to constantly check stores for new merchandise, and once you're there it's a battle royale between you and the other customers. People furiously tear through clothing racks, hoping to get their hands on that one gem before the next person does. From afar, it eerily resembles animals of prey tearing at a fresh carcass, reaching their jaws toward that prime piece of meat before one of its carnivorous neighbors grabs it. It's all about ruthlessness and speed, and that's not a fun shopping experience for anyone.

The solution? Vintage Pal, an online community of elderly people from around the world with wardrobes any halfway decent thrifter would desire. With Vintage Pal, you're not just making a one-off purchase for an article of clothing from an old person—you could use eBay for that. The idea of Vintage Pal is that you can bid to secure an exclusive relationship with the old person of your choice. You can of course browse the person's entire wardrobe to make sure it's worth buying into. Naturally, the Vintage Pal (old person) with the most desirable wardrobe will have their price driven up. Each Vintage Pal will be required to write up a will that leaves their wardrobe (and any agreed upon accessories) to the highest bidder when they pass away. So the real strategy behind choosing the right Vintage Pal is about picking one whose bed could become their deathbed at any moment. Like any investment, it's a risk. What if that person lives years beyond what he was expected to? What if she falls into a coma and their family refuses to pull the plug? But for any dedicated thrifter, the chance for a completely exclusive, truly vintage wardrobe is totally worth it.

Business lesson: Always make sure the reward you're offering is worth the risk.

James Franco Syndrome
(Or, The Time Mark Cuban Gave Me Life Advice)

On the morning of my twenty-fifth birthday, I woke to a nagging voice in my head reminding me of all the things I've yet to accomplish. *Why don't you have a million dollars? Why have you never been to Asia? Why haven't you scrubbed the toilet bowl since you moved in?* I turned on my phone and was greeted by a text message from a friend that read, "Congrats, you're halfway to fifty."

Desperate, I decided to reach out to the one person I knew who could deliver some reassuring words: Mark Cuban. I was introduced to Mark, the billionaire businessman, investor, NBA team owner, and TV personality, when he was interviewed for Elite Daily, and we'd kept a semiregular conversation going for a short time after. I figured if anyone could understand the pressure of that inner voice constantly urging me to do more and be better, it'd be him. After all, the man has built a multi-billion-dollar brand by being ruthlessly competitive and hard on himself.

The last quote he gave for the interview about his key to success was, "I work harder than you. I am more competitive than you. I hate to lose more than you. I will do everything I can in business to kick your ass and that will never change."

A quote like that could only come from a man who's battled with a few contentious voices of his own.

I opened up Gmail and typed happily away.

Hey Mark,

I wanted to reach out on a personal level. I just turned twenty-five. As an obsessive, self-analytical, and most of all, passionate young professional, I was wondering what you would tell your twenty-five-year-old self if you could. I really appreciate it.
Greg

I clicked send and immediately felt better.

That persistent, pessimistic voice that led me to randomly e-mail a billionaire for advice is a symptom of what I've come to call James Franco Syndrome, which, in medical-speak, is an obsessive desire to accomplish as much as possible in the shortest amount of time. And who better than James Franco to epitomize this desire? Aside from being James Franco the movie star and director, he's also James Franco the writer, having published multiple poetry collections, a book of short stories, a novel, and probably a hundred other books I don't even know about. He's also the official face of Gucci's fragrance line for men. He hosted the Oscars, and he seemed to be high the entire time (quite a feat). He teaches classes at NYU, UCLA, USC, and even at Palo Alto High School. He also has degrees from UCLA, Columbia University, NYU, Brooklyn College, and Warren Wilson College, and he's a PhD student at Yale. He also attended Rhode Island School of Design and was accepted to the University of Houston but chose not to attend. He's in a band. He starred in the Broadway production of *Of Mice and Men*. And while it could be easy to argue that he's spreading himself too thin, he seems to juggle all of his commitments with relative ease.

Most people who know me see my compulsive, overbearing approach to life as determination and drive, which, to a degree, it is. I don't want to be good at just one thing. Those people who are less worried about offending me call it overachieving. As my ex-girlfriend put it: "You can't be the best at every single thing you're passionate about, asshole."

Luckily my girlfriend, Brittany, is a bit more understanding. As long as she remains a main course on an overcrowded plate, she supports everything I do. She gets why I work such long hours and take on more than I can seemingly handle; a list that currently includes, but is not limited to, pleasing millions of Elite Daily readers, writing a book, traveling internationally to speak at media conferences, training for a marathon with no plans to actually run a marathon, reading books by only female authors for three consecutive months, and teaching myself the basics of American Sign Language.

She even let me figure out on my own, after months of time-consuming preparation, that making a photo book featuring random dog shit dressed up as everyday characters—poolice officers and poopetrators, the poosident of the Poonited States, and an assortment of other poodestrians walking their poodles—was not the genius idea I originally thought it to be. She did draw the line when I proposed a backup idea of dressing the poop as celebrities and staging movie scenes. Who wouldn't want to see a handcrafted poop replica of Leonardo Di Craprio in *The Great Shatsby*, or a full recreation of the cast of *One Flew Over the Poo Poo's Nest*?*

Another symptom of James Franco Syndrome is the need for validation. Recently, I made it a goal to get verified on Twitter, no matter what it took. There's not a college degree or job title out there that tops the worth of that tiny blue check mark. (Who knew a small, digital symbol would one day have the power to turn a 140-character rant about cargo shorts and cheese into a national conversation?)

Within months, the opportunity presented itself when Twitter announced that members of the Elite Daily editorial team would be getting verified. When I found out I was one of

---

* Other poop names include Bradley Pooper, Cate Blanshit, Shartin Scorsese, Charlie Craplin, Brad Shit, Whitney Pooston, Poopita Nyong'o, Walt Shitman, Edgar Allen Poo, Abraham Stinkin, Adolf Shitler, leader of the Turd Reich, Vladimir Pootin Crapula, *To Kill a Mocking Turd*, *Forrest Dump*, *Bravefart*, *21 Dump Street*, *The Desharted*, *A Tale of Two Shitties*.

those members, I nearly pissed myself. But on official verification day, mine was the only blue check mark that never appeared. I watched everyone else exchange high fives and hugs, relishing the fact they'd just been deemed important members of society.

I spent the weeks following in utter distress. I told everyone I knew about my misfortune, including my eighty-six-year-old grandfather who has never used a computer in his life.

"Trust me," I assured him. "Being verified on Twitter is, like, the most valuable thing that can happen to a person."

I was reliving fifth grade all over again, when my school handed out monthly awards to "top performing" students in the form of bumper stickers that read "Birchwood Booster." Even as kids, we understood these stickers were like peewee-league soccer trophies and everyone would get one. But the school year was nearly over and my bumper sticker was nowhere to be found.

I could hardly bring myself to get in the car with my parents. Driving around Huntington, Long Island, was like swimming in a sea of Birchwood Booster stickers. Every car had a glaring blue sticker on the bumper or back windshield. Our car was bare and meaningless.

Eventually, I did wake up to the blue check mark next to my name. I stared at it the way I'd stare at a father I'd never known. *I've yearned for you, and now you show up unexpectedly in my life*, I thought. *Fine, I'll accept you.* I also ended up getting the Birchwood Booster bumper sticker in the last month of the school year. I'm well aware of the damaging effects of James Franco Syndrome. Among the symptoms already listed, there is also difficulty letting go of failure, a need to study things that don't pertain to what I do, trouble sitting still, and the inability to wear sweatpants in public. Though that last one might just be vanity.

So you see, it made sense for me to elicit advice from Mark Cuban, a guy I can only assume is on the James Franco spectrum. He's got like two hundred businesses, stars in a hit TV show, and owns a basketball team. Perhaps you can be ambitious to a fault, but that's not something I want to believe. Why wouldn't I want to do everything and anything I'm capable of? The hard part is not beating myself up over the things I've yet to do. I was hoping Mark (and James, if you're reading this) could provide some soothing insight.

It was late on the night of my twenty-fifth birthday when my phone buzzed to life with a new e-mail alert. It was Mark. He'd responded. I didn't open it right away. I wanted to cherish the moment. I knew one personal e-mail from Mark Cuban would help subdue all the symptoms I'd been experiencing. I'd print it out and frame it, and the next time I didn't succeed right away or the nagging voice became too much of a distraction, I'd glance over at it and say, "You're right, Mark. I will keep my head up and try harder. Thanks for reassuring me of my self-worth."

I climbed into bed and made sure the mood was right before reading the e-mail. I considered lighting candles, but couldn't find any matches.

The e-mail read,

dont use credit cards, keep learning and keep selling
thats what I would say
m

That was it. Nothing more. It wasn't grand. There were no quotable affirmations. It didn't even have any capitalized letters or apostrophes. I read it over and over again, positive there was something I was missing—perhaps a hidden message if I rearranged the letters. Nothing.

I decided to examine it at face value. I didn't have much to sell, but it seemed like sound financial advice. To keep learning was a given. After all, knowledge is power. But there was no way I was going to stop using credit cards. I'd been working hard earning enough points for a free flight, and the voice in my head said I had to visit Asia before I turned twenty-six.

What a Day

My father married the girl next door. Literally.

From the stories I've heard, he kept a close eye on his neighbor—my mother—throughout their teenage years, watching from his window in the house directly next to hers as boyfriends came and went, before ultimately making his move. Clearly, my existence is proof the move paid off.

Despite growing up next-door neighbors, my parents are very different people. My father has a soft-spoken demeanor, usually reserving his words for witty punch lines and insights that require the least number of syllables possible. My mother is the complete opposite, and when comparing my father's quiet disposition to her loud, in your face, blame-it-on-Italian-roots tendencies, it's hard not to assume it was the other way around, that *she* made the move and went after him. Regardless of who gets the credit, it's a fairytale love story, and one that has set the standards fairly high for my own attempts at romance. Luckily,

I've come to realize there's no point in trying to top my parents' origins of love when I can instead ride its coattails. The story of their neighborly romance has become a go-to topic of conversation on first dates, and it works like a charm. After all, I am the spawn of two hometown soul mates. Who wouldn't trust that I turned out right?

Though the biggest advantage of having parents that grew up next door to each other isn't that it's a shameless icebreaker. The real perk was growing up with two sets of grandparents who live next door to each other. (Not two sets exactly, considering my father never knew his father, but you get my point.)

After I was born, my parents moved to a town only ten minutes away from where they grew up, so visits to my grand-parents' respective homes were frequent. By the time it took to decide which song to listen to on the radio we would have already arrived, both houses standing quaint and inviting next to one another. It was my own personal sanctuary, and it spanned the length of two front lawns. Looking on from the street, my mother's parents, Nanny and Pop as we called them, lived in the house to the left. My father's mother, Grammy, to the right. It was my choice as to which house I'd want to enter first, guaranteed to get spoiled with freshly prepared meals and crisp dollar bills in each. I was living every child's fantasy.

My girlfriend, Brittany, whose parents also happen to be hometown sweethearts, experienced an even more tight-knit family geography growing up. The house she grew up in is across the street from her grandparents' house. Next door to her grandparents' house is the house her grandfather grew up in. A few houses down is her aunt's house. A few more houses over are her cousins, and even more cousins live on the next street over. Her family takes the *Everybody Loves Raymond* gag to an entirely new level. Though even she would have to travel a few states over to see her other set of grandparents.

Growing up with such favorable circumstances meant that I always had two sets of support systems close by. This support was especially beneficial when life transitioned from playdates and scraped knees to SATs and overly dramatic high-school heartbreaks. When I lost a varsity lacrosse game or couldn't understand why my parents wouldn't let me do whatever it was I wanted to do, I'd take the short drive over to my grandparents' houses, the distance between them appearing even closer than when I was a child. I'd spend hours abandoning the weight of adolescence by playing cards at Nanny and Pop's or being a volunteer food taster at Grammy's. Even as a college student I felt the same childlike excitement each time I stepped out of my car and took in the comforting sight of the two houses side by side.

While I'd always appreciated the convenience of my grandparents living next door to each other, my understanding of just how much I'd come to depend on their one, central location came later, when I was a junior in college. In 2009, Nanny began a long battle with lung cancer, and in late 2010 she was moved from her house to hospice care. Like so many families, mine became even stronger the day she was diagnosed. What I had the hardest time facing was the fact that the dynamics of my perfect setup—me at point a and my grandparents' two homes, teeming with life and separated only by a sliver of driveway, at point b—had been altered for the first time. It was unnerving knowing my grandmother wasn't where she'd always been my whole life.

Nanny ended up passing away shortly after she moved to hospice care with most of my family by her side. It was a peaceful departure, the kind of death that allows you to still eat a full meal after the funeral at whatever local restaurant has a big enough back room to fit your entire family. This meal doesn't stem at all from a place of insensitivity. It's simply a sign that a full life has been lived, and that alone is something worth celebrating. I hope when my time comes people can't wait to stuff their faces with pasta once I'm in the ground.

Only a few months after Nanny's passing, it was Grammy's turn to venture from the setting with which I'd always associated her. After a bad fall and resulting hip surgery, she was moved into a nursing home. It was at that moment I realized my childhood place of serenity—the same place my parents first tried on each other's love to see how it would fit, the place where I'd spent countless weekends as a child running from house to house to equally distribute my time between grandparents—had officially been dismantled on both sides.

Visits to Grammy's nursing home were harsh reminders that things had changed. Not to mention I was genuinely frightened by the place. I'd never liked hospitals (even though my father has worked in one all my life), and I found the nursing home to be even worse. The hallways were stale and colorless, with sporadic, gargling coughs and the crackle of oxidized joints that reverberated through the walls like carnival rides just getting started. Hospitals at least house diversity. One person could be dying from gunshot wounds, but only one wing over a child has just taken its first breath in a new mother's arms. Nursing homes are depressingly monotonous.

I also couldn't help but feel overly protective when visiting Grammy. I'd see other old ladies with the same thinning, disheveled hair and cloudy eyes. They'd have identical wrinkles across the same loose-skinned knuckles and an all-too-familiar pattern of veins winding up their legs. But they weren't my grandmothers. Grammy was different, I'd tell myself, and it pained me to think someone else would even place her in the same category as the others.

I always just assumed her stay in the nursing home would be temporary. I figured that once she was back home we could rebuild the structure we'd lost. It'd never be the same without Nanny, but at least there'd be two sides to even out the scale again. One grandparent on each side would be enough to hold the fabric of my childhood together.

One night following Grammy's admittance to the nursing home, I had a strange dream that her house, along with Nanny's and Pop's, melted. Slow drip by slow drip, the two homes simultaneously formed shiny, metallic puddles in the unforgiving summer sun. I woke up the next morning drenched in sweat, as if I'd actually been there, collecting the heat and beginning to melt myself. The dream reinforced my fear that if the familiarity of my grandparents' homes faded, the memories somehow would, too. I was desperate to conserve the convenience of the location and pass it down to generations after me, like a museum artifact or piece of rare art. I had visions of one day buying both houses, moving my parents into one and my future wife's parents into the other, just so my future kids could have the same accessibility to their grandparents I had.

Months after the dream, memories took on an even greater meaning in my life. It was no longer the fear of my childhood memories vanishing that took center stage, though—it was the reality that Grammy's memories were actually starting to disappear. We first noticed something was off when she began repeating questions during visits. It started with simple questions like "What did you do today?" or "How is school going?" She'd ask, listen intently while nodding along, then, a few minutes later, ask the same exact question, as if she weren't happy with the first answer and was offering a chance at redemption.

At first, I blamed fatigue for her cloudy memory. I'd look around the small room, sunlight barely creeping through the window, her teeth in a tall glass of water on the nightstand, and imagine I wouldn't be the sharpest person in that setting either. Though I knew the issue was not to be taken lightly when I noticed her impressive reading output go from one book a week to hardly one page a day. In her healthier years, she had the ability to read more quickly than anyone I'd ever met. Each time I'd visit her as a child, she'd have a new hardcover book from the library bookmarked and sitting on her coffee table. Hundreds and hundreds of pages a week that stood no chance against her. People would always bring her books to the nursing home as gifts, and I took tally each week as their unread pages began to stack up on her nightstand like a miniature city skyline.

Doctors officially diagnosed her with dementia after the repetition began making its way into every conversation. She wasn't even able to recall who had visited her earlier in the day. Once when my entire family was visiting, she announced she needed to use the bathroom. We waited patiently in the room and when the bathroom door swung back open her face lit up with genuine astonishment. "What a surprise!" she cheered. "I haven't seen you in so long. So sorry you came while I was using the toilet."

Luckily it was only her short-term memory that was affected. With each visit I'd test her thoroughly, making sure my childhood was still intact and vibrant in her mind. We'd recall the funny stories we wrote together, the vocabulary words she would test me on when I was younger, and all the recipes she'd brought to life for my family over the years. We'd have the same conversation at least five times during one visit, but it didn't bother me. It was refreshing to relive the moments that had shaped our relationship throughout the years.

What I loved most was that she'd always remember how passionate I was about writing, and with each visit, she told the same exact story of her father, who worked as a newspaper journalist for an English paper in Puerto Rico. She'd go on for minutes at a time about his ability to write and how captivating of a storyteller he was. She'd explain that during the holidays the entire family and all the kids would huddle around him, hanging on to every single syllable that slipped out of his mouth. Without fail, she'd finish the story by boasting about how he was good friends with Joe DiMaggio, because even the greatest baseball player in the world loved my grandfather's stories. Each time, I left her side with a renewed sense of purpose.

I eventually found out through my parents that Grammy had been aware of her impending dementia early on. She'd started staying home more often a few years prior to her eventual diagnosis. She'd even opted out of Christmas Eve dinner at my family's house. At the time I hadn't even noticed, but now it made me sick to my stomach to think of her afraid and alone, desperate to hide any hint of her mind's deterioration from us.

I thought of my own selfish fears. The notion that I'd somehow lose a piece of my childhood if my grandparents' homes didn't stay forever intact and stable next to one another was an impractical one, brought on by my mind's irrational tendency to place the burden of existential fears onto something tangible. When I was younger I was convinced that if I didn't say good night to my family they'd cease to exist while I slept. I also believed that if I didn't pray before bed my house would set on fire. I'm not sure where that particular dread came from, but I think the Catholic church would be proud.

Then I thought of Grammy's fears. Legitimate fears. The fear of actually losing her memories. For years she must have woken up unsure if that particular day would be the day her forgetfulness transformed into something far more damaging. Forgetting what she had for dinner the night before was saddening but manageable, I'm sure. But the constant fear of one day forgetting her family members or even her own childhood must have weighed more heavily on her than anything else.

In the nursing home, she was past the point of fearful anticipation. Like riding a roller coaster, she had been most aware and afraid on the way up, preparing for a sudden drop that she could only sense but not quite see in front of her. Once she was past the initial free fall and her dementia was full-fledged, she was simply along for the ride. There was a strange sense of comfort in knowing she was at least free of the fear.

Then there were my parents, the ones who'd actually grown up in those two homes I'd learned to cherish so much. Their fear and emotions surrounding this huge change must have been devastating, yet I was the one wallowing in angst over inevitability instead of taking the time to consider the new memories I could still make with Grammy.

I was able to enjoy a beautiful spring afternoon with Grammy a few months before she passed away. It was the first warm day of the season and my family decided it would be nice to take her outside to enjoy the weather. We helped her out of bed and into her wheelchair and made our way to the nursing home's courtyard. Surprisingly, the courtyard was extremely well-kept, flush with blooming flowers and dense, vibrant foliage that blocked the view of the looming brick building. Compared to the stark hallways and cramped rooms inside the nursing-home walls it was a true oasis. We were the only ones outside and we took our time wheeling Grammy around the narrow cobblestone path. At that point her mind would refresh almost instantly, and every few feet it was as if she'd just stepped outside for the very first time. "What a day. It's so beautiful," she'd repeat without fail. It was the perfect commentary for the moment, and none of us would have ever gotten tired of it, no matter how many laps we took around the courtyard.

As we prepared to make our way back inside I took a long hard look at my family. My brother stood close by me, as shocked as I was that a setting so gorgeous could be affiliated with the very place that made us feel so uneasy with each visit. My mother strolled slowly next to my father as he pushed Grammy's wheelchair. She was leading the pack, with a blanket draped over her lap and one of the biggest smiles I'd ever seen. I tried to envision the first time my father realized a cute girl was living next door. I pictured their first date, which they've told me was to a softball game. I thought about the initial doubts they must have had, questioning whether or not it was possible that the person they were meant to be with forever could really be the person that's been right there—right next door—all along. I imagined my mother meeting Grammy for the first time, slowly becoming more than just the girl next door. I thought of how nervous my father must have been meeting Nanny and Pop. I felt warm picturing Grammy introducing herself to Nanny and Pop not just as a neighbor, but as something more. "It's so beautiful," Grammy chirped from her wheelchair.

I knew that once Grammy was settled back upstairs in her room she wouldn't even remember that she had been outside. She'd forget the warmth of the sun and the smell of the trees. She wouldn't recall that she saw my family and me. The day would all be one empty space in her mind. But it didn't matter that she wouldn't remember the day. Luckily, the important thing about memories, whether they change with time or disappear completely, is that they happened. I knew the feeling of that day would last forever, and that was enough for me.

My Summer as a Pick-Up Artist

It was a spring night in New York City as I surveyed the open-seating section of an outdoor bar with my best friend Phil. Like so many of the other men around us fueled by the warm seasonal breeze and alcohol, we were searching for women.

Generally, the strategy behind selecting which girl to approach is as arbitrary as it is animalistic. Whether it's the first girl a guy sees or the girl who looks most receptive to conversing with a stranger, there's usually only surface-level rationalization involved. That night, though, we weren't interested in which girls would be easiest to approach. We were in pursuit of the biggest challenge.

Phil had been studying the "science" of pick-up artistry for months, and that night he was prepared to show me "The Cube" technique for the first time. The cube is a personality exercise of sorts. The idea is to tell a girl that you could accurately describe her personality by asking a series of questions. You then recite blatant generalizations based on her answers, which more often than not, she'd perceive as detailed understandings of her own personality. It's not all that different than the curbside hustlers with novelty crystal balls and handwritten signs that advertise five-dollar psychic readings. My only job was to tag along and not screw anything up.

We settled on a table of three girls and three guys. Phil wasted no time. "I have to ask, do you believe in psychic intuition?" he interrupted. "I know this is random, but I bet I can tell you everything about your personality." He focused on the girls, ignoring the guys altogether.

"So prove it," one of them responded. Phil motioned for her to put her hands in his and instructed her to close her eyes. Before he could even get started, the guys said they had to go and left the table without acknowledging us.

"Imagine a cube," Phil began. "How big is it? What color? Now imagine a ladder. How many rungs? Now a horse. What kind and color? There's a storm. What kind of storm?" And so on and so on with similarly inane, ludicrous questions. All the while, one of the girl's friends nudged me playfully, assuming I had been privy to this show before.

When the questions concluded, the girl slowly opened her eyes, readjusting to the world around her. For the next two minutes, I sat in awe as Phil interpreted each one of her answers without missing a beat.

"The cube represents you," he said. Since she described her cube as being small, it meant that at times she was an introvert.

Her cube was on the ground, so Phil told her she was well-grounded. The ladder represented her friends, and since she described it as having only a few rungs, it meant she had a select few friends that she really cared about. The horse was her ideal man. She picked a stallion, which meant she wanted a masculine partner. And the horse's color was white, so she also desired someone that could be sensitive and emotionally stable.

With each interpretation, which was nothing more than a series of basic abstractions, she grew more wide-eyed. "You're describing her perfectly," one of her friends shouted. By the end of the night, the three guys had never returned. As the girl entered her number into Phil's phone, she explained that she had a boyfriend, but that she didn't know where the relationship was going. One of her friends gave me her number, and with that, we left as suddenly as we'd arrived.

I was first introduced to pick-up artistry when Phil, following the end of a four-year relationship, turned to books on seduction to help heal his heartbreak. Like many before him, he was directed to Neil Strauss's *New York Times* best seller *The Game: Penetrating the Secret Society of Pickup Artists*. As critiqued as it's been worshipped, *The Game* is a memoir that profiles the now mainstream personality Neil Strauss's rise from loser to ladies' man through the mastery of the highly controversial and taboo culture of pick-up artistry.

There is an entire underground culture of men that dedicate their nights to learning the science behind attracting women. These men are not born alpha males that light up rooms with their charisma and physique. These men are average, usually dorky dudes who, by following a set of well-practiced rules, are able to intrigue and even sleep with women who would otherwise overlook them.

After *The Game*, Phil devoured any related text he could get his hands on, from Robert Greene's *The Art of Seduction*, to W. Anton's *The Manual: What Women Want and How to Give It to Them*, to sales books about persuasion and FBI manuals about body language. He was consumed by the notion that if he read enough about what women wanted to hear, speaking and embodying those tactics would become second nature.

At first I dismissed the idea that there could be any legitimacy within the books Phil left lingering around our apartment. I never had any issues connecting with women, and the concepts that he presented seemed like the complete opposite of anything I'd ever done to attract a girl.

"A neg," he explained, "is a backhanded compliment. It's important to slightly offend the girl you're interested in. Or at least to not show immediate interest."

"How does that make sense?" I asked half-heartedly, not sure I really wanted to know the answer.

"Next time you go out, watch how every guy interacts with the best-looking girl. 'Can I buy you a drink?' 'What's your name?' 'You're really pretty.' The most attractive girls never have to work for affection, so they can't help but want the guy that makes his presence known but doesn't pursue them."

Conversations like these became commonplace, and each time I found myself paying closer attention. It was our first summer living on our own in New York City, and like Phil, I too was recovering from the fallout of a four-year relationship. Breakups have a funny way of changing people in the first few months following the split. Some people go skydiving. Others get makeovers and chop off their hair. My ex-girlfriend got a tattoo the size of her torso and took up pole dancing. I, whether I knew it at the time or not, would spend the entire summer of 2012 becoming a pick-up artist—and a good one at that.

I was only a few chapters into *The Game* when Phil decided I was ready for my first real taste of "gaming," as it's called. We were at a rooftop bar for a friend's birthday when he assured me I'd be leaving with the phone number of a gorgeous waitress he'd spotted. "I'll open, then you neg," he instructed. An "open" referred to the initial approach, which was meant to gain the target's interest without displaying immediate signs of attraction. I felt extremely unprepared.

When the waitress made her way to the corner of the bar to catch her breath, we approached. "We've been debating about something all night and we wanted to get your opinion," Phil said. "Our friend got in an argument with his girlfriend the other night because she got drunk and kissed a girl. He thinks it's cheating, she says it's not."

This was all a devised lie of course, but it was my job to play along. Whatever her opinion was, Phil would take the opposite stance. When she said she thought the imaginary girl in our scenario was cheating, I playfully boasted that she'd sided with me. Then, without even thinking, I threw in my neg.

"You look like the type of girl who hooks up with other girls when you're drunk." My insides tightened as the words slipped from my mouth. I'd never say that to anyone, let alone a girl I was interested in. To my surprise, she laughed and stroked the length of my arm while chuckling. "No way, silly. I like guys." This touch was referred to by pick-up artists as "kino," as in kinesthetic—a friendly touch that signifies the girl's interest and comfort.

I ended my first official night of gaming with a number from the waitress, whom I found out was six years older than I was. As I said my good-byes, I watched out of the corner of my eye as Phil locked lips with a woman at the bar. It all seemed too good to be true.

The following months would prove to be the most social of my life. Looking back, I have a difficult time determining where the social experiment ended and the full-blown obsession began.

Phil and I would spend nights repeating rules as if they were biblical:

Never buy a girl a drink, make her buy you a drink.
Never give a girl your number, make her give you hers.
Always approach from the side, not directly from the front.
Make sure your body language makes it appear as if you're going
   to leave at any moment.

By the time mid-July rolled around, we considered ourselves highly skilled at winning the attention of pretty much any girls we wanted. When we told our friends they laughed at the idea, until we'd prove it to them. The first time I brought a friend out to game I ended up with an invite home from a thirty-year-old woman, who moments before was showing me pictures of her kids and "baby daddy."

Another night, a friend challenged Phil and me to game in a restaurant. Phil intercepted a woman dining with her boyfriend when she got up to go to the bathroom. I got a text later the same night from the girl I met after joining her and her friends at their table. It read, "I can't pick out a bathing suit for tomorrow. If I send pictures will you help me pick one out?"

Once in a salsa club downtown, I approached a stunning professional dancer who had a line of men waiting for a trial run with her. After I asked her if she was an amateur dancer just learning the style, we ended up on the dance floor, laughing as I tried to learn the steps. I found myself meeting girls while waiting for the girl I was supposed to be on a date with. I spent nights under the stars on strange rooftops, and one morning woke up in an apartment in Greenwich Village with a note that read, "I trust you," on top of a key.

That summer, gaming became the only form of interaction with the opposite sex Phil and I knew. Though our methods were a peculiar combination of the many philosophies we'd adopted, one guideline truly drove the success: have no fear of rejection.

We forced ourselves to confront rejection using the three-second rule: we'd commit to approaching beautiful women within three seconds of seeing them, which forced us to engage in conversation immediately, never allowing our minds enough time to develop excuses and worst-case scenarios. By embracing rejection as a normal part of life, we, in turn, exuded an undeniable aura of confidence. Plus, we were armed with enough openings, negs, and closing lines to fill a novel.

The routine became mathematical. I could critique a girl's nail polish and she'd end up all over me. Phil became a master at spending nights strategically chatting with the friends of the girl he was interested in, completely ignoring her altogether. This, of course, resulted in the girl fighting for his attention. We could predict when girls would let their guards down. We knew exactly when they'd provide a touch or a laugh. We spent the entire summer with the women that the guys around us wished they could be with.

It was sublime. It was transcendental. And by the time the summer was over and the chilling fall breeze made itself known, I'd realized it was terrible.

What was intended to be experimental and harmless had become a programmed and systematic habit. Phil couldn't walk outside or ride a train without approaching a new target. My phone book had become a dense collection of numbers with names I didn't remember. Some of the girls we'd meet with again, but most were one-time results of the game at work.

Worst of all, my view of women had become severely skewed. While the confidence I had gained was a great and important feat in itself, it was depressing that the tactics I was using were delusory. I had learned how to get women to fall for me within minutes of speaking to them, but the success was fueled by dishonesty, rudeness, and characteristics I had never intended to acquire. The line between seduction and deception was dangerously blurred.

In the beginning, Phil explained that attraction lies in the idea of pursuit, which is why so many of the women we intentionally didn't show attraction toward so greatly desired us. But the entire concept became meaningless once I realized that through gaming, I had lost the excitement of the pursuit. Even when we did meet girls we were interested in getting to know on a personal level, we couldn't help but put on the disguises we'd become so comfortable wearing. I was living in New York City with a roster of more willing girls than I knew what to do with yet I felt lonelier than I ever had.

By October, I had stopped myself from going out as much. I figured alone time could help remedy the whirlwind experience of the summer. I needed my cube to be small.

One night I was walking into the gym when I ran into a familiar face. It was a girl from my hometown, though we'd never said a single word to each other despite going to high school together for four years. We shared an awkward hello and that night I decided I'd reach out to her on Facebook and ask her to grab a drink sometime soon.

We ended up getting together a week later, catching each other up on our lives, and in a strange way, meeting for the first time. On our second date, we ended up on the couch in her apartment. I explained to her that I had the ability to tell her everything about her personality and instructed her to put her hands in mine. She did, but with hesitation. As I went through the motions, asking her the series of obscure questions, it became increasingly obvious that she could see right through the entire bit. Suddenly the whole act sounded stupid and contrived, because it was. By the end of my performance I admitted to her that it was just a dumb pick-up artist trick I had learned from a friend.

For the rest of the night we laughed together, equally astonished at how I ended up in her apartment six years after high school. Nerves shot through my body and butterflies tore through my stomach—something I hadn't felt in a long time.

I could have gone in for the kiss right then and there, but I decided not to. I figured there was no rush. And as I crawled in bed solo that night, I noticed that for the first time since the beginning of the summer, I didn't feel so alone.

Bridging the Gap

Growing up, I had the straightest teeth of anyone I knew. I'd receive compliments all the time from strangers who would stop to admire my smile as if it were something rare and mythical. So I was shocked the day the orthodontist told me I'd need not only braces, but a palate expander, too. The palate expander, he explained, was a device that would be mounted to the roof of my mouth and, using a manual crank, would gradually widen my upper jaw. In turn, a gap the width of my pinky finger would appear between my two front teeth.

He assured me that even though my teeth appeared straight at the moment, they'd shift later in life. As a seventh grader with limited time to establish a lasting reputation before high school, I demanded to know what "later in life" meant. Would I be thirty years old? Forty? I made every effort to convince my parents I'd be married by then, and would have a binding agreement that assumed my wife would stay with me for better or worse. I figured if my teeth shifting a little would be the worst problem in this hypothetical marriage, I'd be in pretty good shape.

My parents ended up listening to the man with the PhD and intellectual-looking bald spot. My determined fate was several gap-toothed months with the palate expander followed by three years with braces. In my mind, I was a perfectly good car in the hands of a mechanic with nothing better to do than tamper with parts just so he had something to fix.

The most astonishing thing about braces is how suddenly they become part of your life. One day you're playing outside with friends, then the next day you're strapped to a reclining chair getting metal cemented into your mouth. It's a stark reminder that life isn't all fun and games. After all, braces are never a kid's choice. This is funny considering plenty less fortunate people in the world would kill for even one trip to the dentist. Luckily, once we kids who grew up with braces reach a certain age, we realize there's no point in complaining about the fact our parents spent thousands of dollars to ensure our teeth fit society's staunch standards of beauty. When you're a kid, though, braces have no positive outcome. They are social suicide, and that is all.

Of course, before I even got my braces I'd have to survive life with its much less talked about cousin, the palate expander. Hearing the phrases "gap tooth" and "facial alterations" slip out of the orthodontist's mouth as if they were everyday words in a casual conversation made me feel sick. Though in his defense, there's no easy way to tell a kid entering the most crucial stage of puberty that his face is about to resemble David Letterman's if he were to get stung by a hundred bees and punched repeatedly in the mouth by Mike Tyson.

Once the palate expander was in place, talking and eating immediately became a struggle, and it wasn't long before I pretty much gave up both altogether. My face thinned out noticeably after a few weeks, and I resorted to nods and closed-mouth grins as my primary forms of communication. Other parents would approach my mom at church and after-school events, wondering if I'd become ill. It wasn't the easiest question to ask a mother, but there was no denying that I looked like I was withering away, struck by a rare disease or depressed.

What was even worse was the fact that any food I did try to eat would get stuck in the small space between the palate expander and the roof of my mouth. My parents alternated shifts scraping out the food remnants by hand. It wasn't easy to get excited about much knowing that later in the day my own mother's fingers would be halfway down my throat as she struggled to see how much half-chewed hamburger meat was rotting between my palate and the jagged metal surface.

Though there was nothing I dreaded more than the manual crank. The way the device actually did its job and expanded was by placing a thin metal key into a tiny screw hole on its bottom side and completing one full rotation. This cranking shifted my teeth and expanded my upper jaw, and each time it left a stinging pressure that floated along my top row of teeth like a dense fog. It was also a task my parents had to complete twice a day. They'd apologize sincerely each time another rotation was completed, and I did everything in my power not to blame them.

By the time the gap reached its full potential I'd become a full-blown mute. My grades suffered and my social life was depleted. My parents held meetings with my teachers to explain why my participation had gone from stellar to nonexistent. I'd spend nights in front of the bathroom mirror examining my gap, hoping it wouldn't widen any more than it already had. I even scribbled down the names of all the Egyptian gods I'd learned about in history class on a piece of paper so I could recite a prayer to each. Though I backed out at the last minute, afraid that word would somehow get back to my Catholic parents.

Navigating the school hallways was like walking through a minefield. I'd do my best to avoid the girls I thought were cute and the guys the cute girls thought were cute. It wasn't like I could hide the fact my face had changed shape and I could use a sock to floss between my two front teeth, but I tried anyway. Most of the kids were respectful of my unfortunate circumstances. They'd make obvious attempts to hold eye contact or leave me with sympathetic pats on the shoulder. A few would try to lighten the mood with jokes, but often that would backfire. My lowest point came when a friend told me that my new mouth was cool because it looked like the Predator's. I hadn't seen the movie, but once I searched pictures online I was devastated, especially since the comparison wasn't too far off.

When I was even younger, in fifth grade, I experienced a full year of having terrible stomach pains every morning before school. My parents took me to a therapist who described what I was feeling as social anxiety. I'd sit with the therapist once a week. During most visits she'd ask me to create scenes using the various toys she had stockpiled in her office. Eventually, by what I assume to have been exercises to address the scenarios and fears that existed in my head, and not necessarily the real world, I was able to get over the stomachaches and even get excited about going to school. It was shortly after the Predator comparison that I started to feel the familiar sharp pains cut across my torso again.

This pain caused me to constantly beg my parents to take days off from school. "I just don't have it in me today," I'd say, but most of the time I was given a stern "no."

My parents had always told me that if I really wanted something, I'd have to make a strong case for it. So when I had the idea of being homeschooled for the rest of the year, I presented a well-thought-out list with the pros outweighing the cons. Again, I received a quick "no."

"Just own it," they'd tell me. "It's just one very small part of your life."

Easy to say when you don't have a medieval-style torture device cemented to the roof of your mouth, I'd think to myself.

Shortly after my denial of homeschool, I was sitting in the cafeteria at school when a friend at my table asked me what it felt like to all of a sudden turn ugly. He didn't ask the question in a spiteful way. He seemed to be generally interested more than anything, but the question still hurt. Mostly because it was the question I'd been asking myself since the first day I noticed a slight separation appearing between my teeth.

Years later, when my palate expander would eventually be removed and I'd finish my three-year prison sentence with braces, I started to acknowledge all the lessons I'd learned from that period of my life. It's easy to talk about how difficult times made you a stronger person long after those difficult times are over. Though, I like to think I was onto something in that moment at the cafeteria table, because instead of answering my friend's question, I stood up from the table and motioned for everyone to do the same. Without hesitation I filled my mouth with chocolate milk and forcefully filtered it back out through my gap. The steady brown stream shot through my teeth like a faulty sprinkler head and splashed gracefully across the table. This provoked an eruption of applause from my friends, along with echoing chants of "Do it again."

Before I could raise the milk carton to my mouth for a refill, a teacher that had seen the whole thing ran over and pulled me aside.

"You're going to have to come with me to the dean's office," he instructed. "But not before you clean that up."

Then he leaned in close and admitted, "That was pretty cool though."

I headed back to the lunch table with a handful of paper towels and a gap-toothed smile that lit up the room. I wasn't worried about receiving detention. After all, it would just be one very small part of my life.

For the Kids

I'm one of those people who are overcome with fear the moment something good happens. It's a fear tied to the idea that in any natural cycle of life failure follows success, the way death supersedes life. All great empires fall. Every star burns out. No sports dynasty can win forever. So when I do accomplish something worth celebrating, I tend to contain my excitement to the point people urge me to let loose and celebrate. But I can't. If anything, I grip on to my invisible rope even tighter, preparing for the floor to crumble beneath my feet.

To be clear, I'm aware becoming fearful after success is not a healthy way of existing. But if you're wondering, I'm working on it. Living in the moment is essential. It's all we've really got. Though, prior to any of that self-awareness, I used to think filling the space after an accomplishment with good deeds would buy me more time before something tragic occurred.

As a child, I volunteered often. Not by choice, but because my parents dragged me along with them. Every year around Thanksgiving we'd help collect food for underprivileged families at my local church. I'd spend hours organizing all the food people dropped off. My mouth would water as I separated cans of green beans from corn, made toppling mountains of cranberry sauce, and carried giant turkeys to a freezer. At that age, it didn't necessarily feel rewarding, but as I got older I learned to appreciate the experience. It's also when I started to believe that all that childhood volunteering had something to do with my life turning out pretty smoothly up to that point, as if I'd done the opposite of sell my soul to the devil. Can you sell your soul to the patron saint of volunteering for the guarantee of a halfway decent life? I doubt the good guys barter like that, but it didn't stop me from believing that carrying all those turkeys back and forth had a positive effect on things.

Once I moved away to college, it became difficult to make it back home to the Thanksgiving food collection. Though one year, just before a particularly challenging round of finals, I got the urge to volunteer on my own. It was a combination of the holiday spirit and the feeling of needing to refuel my good-deed gas tank, which really means that I thought it'd bring me luck on my finals. I ended up volunteering at a soup kitchen in Harlem later that week through a program offered at my college. It was a fulfilling experience, and at the same time, I felt more confident going into my finals.

After the soup kitchen, I didn't volunteer for some time. I graduated from college, moved back in with my parents, and worked a string of terrible retail jobs (including a clothing store and a vitamin shop, though nothing in my life will ever be more trying than working at Toys "R" Us, where kids really do extend their arms airplane style and knock every piece of merchandise off the shelves). When I finally landed a job writing for a website and moved into my own apartment in Astoria, Queens, my life finally felt like it was going well enough to consider volunteering again. With my new successes came the fear of impending failure, creeping in as slow and steady as a soup-kitchen line.

Picking where to volunteer isn't easy. There are the obvious choices like soup kitchens and clothing drives, and you could of course always just donate money somewhere. But I wanted something different. Something that I could call my own. Granted, you probably shouldn't consider a charity based on how it will make you look, but it was my first time volunteering without the help of my family or university, and I wanted it to represent the person I'd become. Or at least the person I thought I'd become.

As fate would have it, I was reading an interview with James Franco one day and he mentioned an organization he was heavily involved with called The Art of Elysium. The organization has volunteers—all artists of some fashion—visit children's hospitals in New York and Los Angeles. Singers would sing with the children, actors would put on shows, and painters would lead elaborate arts and craft sessions. It was like the Hollywood of charity organizations. A list of celebrities who had volunteered or supported the organization in some capacity included Kanye West, Julianne Moore, Matthew McConaughey, Johnny Depp, Jimmy Fallon, Eva Mendes, and too many more to name. Yet I couldn't help but notice there were no writers going to the hospitals to write with the children. What better way to give back than with what I loved to do anyway? I decided to apply as a volunteer.

A couple weeks after applying I headed into Manhattan to meet Kevin, the organization's New York program manager, at a busy Starbucks in Union Square. He would be conducting my interview, to both consider my volunteering desires and make sure I was sane enough to be allowed near children. I imagined I'd be sitting down to meet a social-worker type, someone who would ask the same kinds of questions a psychiatrist would on a first visit. Kevin actually turned out to be not much older than I was. He sported a tight denim jacket and bleached blonde hair, and greeted me with the chipper voice of someone who maintains the same energy level at all times, even when you know they must be tired. He seemed friendly and about as West Coast as a person can be, having just moved from Los Angeles a couple months prior to help expand the organization. I was immediately at ease knowing the meeting would be a conversation, not an interrogation.

After some small talk, I told Kevin my idea about working with kids to help them write.

"And if they aren't up for writing themselves, I could maybe take notes on their stories and write them myself. Maybe even print out the pages and make little books for them and their parents. Or what about a collection of their stories in one big book? Maybe we could even get it published."

The ideas I rattled off all seemed plausible in my mind, though I could tell they were making Kevin uneasy.

"You have to keep in mind, most of these kids have been sick their entire lives," he explained.

Right then I could see how dreamy and romantic my idea must have sounded. I was afraid Kevin now saw me as an amateur writer looking to exploit sick kids for a big break. I sat there speechless, cappuccino in hand, feeling like I'd been caught stealing from a baby.

"Don't get me wrong, it's a thoughtful idea," he added, sensing my discomfort. "It's just that we never want to do anything that will make a child consider their health."

I took a sip of my coffee, trying my best to hide the look of embarrassment that was sweeping across my face. Kevin took the opportunity to drive his point home.

"Imagine that ever since you're old enough to form memories, all you know is hospital beds and weekly surgeries. Imagine only a small sliver of your time each day, or even week, is dedicated to playing and being around other kids. The rest of the time is spent connected to tubes and feeling sick from countless medications. It's terrible what some of these children have to endure, and if we as volunteers can't be sure we're lifting their spirits, then what's our purpose?

"You can of course still volunteer in another capacity," he added. "We can always use people for the group arts and crafts sessions."

There are plenty of moments in life in which you realize you've been seeing only what you want to see, looking way past the reality of a situation. Kevin's words turned the lights on in my head, and just like that it was clear what I hadn't signed up for. It wasn't a chance to feed my artistic ego by parading around saying I volunteered at the same charity as James Franco and Johnny Depp. It definitely wasn't a chance to sharpen my writing skills. What I'd actually signed up for was a chance to put a smile on the faces of sick children. With each new realization the pulsing knot in my stomach grew, and before I knew it, I was excusing myself from the table and heading toward the bathroom.

Looking at my own face in the mirror I contemplated my next move. If I decided to go through with volunteering, I'd have to face two things I have a hard time dealing with in life: hospitals and sick children. The fact I hadn't considered this while applying to be a volunteer at children's hospitals just goes to show how blinded I get by half-thought-out ideas. The truth is I can't even go to a dentist appointment without first taking a trip to the bathroom to give myself a pep talk. (I spend a lot of time talking to myself in bathrooms.) What starts as a fervent, Al Pacino–style pump-up speech always ends up losing steam and heading in the direction of, "Well, if I die, I've done a lot of things and seen a lot of places." It didn't help that during my last dentist appointment, Bob Dylan's "Knockin' on Heaven's Door" started playing on the office radio. I could have sworn the office's bright light in my eyes as I lay in the dentist's chair was a direct path to the afterlife.

Simply walking into a hospital to visit someone makes me queasy with the thought of needles and death and adults eating cafeteria food. Throw a child into the equation and I can barely breathe. I still have to turn away from the scene in *E.T.* when he's dying and hooked up to all those tubes.

I tried my best not to panic and instead laid out my options.

OPTION #1: Tell Kevin I just got a call from work and would have to reschedule our meeting. Of course, I'd leave and never speak to him again.

OPTION #2: Tell Kevin I forgot to mention that I'd recently contracted malaria during a trip to Africa, and that even though I'd stopped showing symptoms, it probably wouldn't be a good idea to be around children just yet. Still a lie, but I'd appear slightly less pathetic in his eyes.

OPTION #3: Go through with it.

I met Kevin back at the table and apologized. I told him that I understood why he had concerns about introducing a writing exercise to the children, and that I'd be open to learning about other ways I could volunteer. We settled on the group arts and crafts session. There'd be a volunteer with expertise in painting who would lead the activity. I'd be like an elf to Santa.

For the next hour Kevin explained the strict cautionary procedures that were required when visiting the children. Direct touching of any kind was to be avoided, and hands had to be washed before entering any room. If you had so much as a sore throat the day you were scheduled to volunteer, you'd have to reschedule. Depending on the child's illness, a mask and gloves could be required. If a child even once said they didn't feel well, the activity would end abruptly. It was crucial to get the child's permission before commencing any activity, since the child had every right to say no.

Running through the professional protocol made me feel even more uneasy knowing that stepping foot inside a hospital was in my near future. Though as Kevin began to discuss the children's daily lives, my angst was pushed aside. Many of the kids, depending on their specific illness, spent most of the time confined to their beds. Most of them had to be homeschooled by their parents in the hospitals, if that was even possible on a daily basis. In time, some of the children would be cured, others were temporary visitors to begin with, but then there were the children who wouldn't see adulthood—the children who wouldn't finish school, find a job, or have a family of their own. I thought of their parents, living each day with no guarantee that tomorrow would ever resemble today, all the while hoping for a yesterday when there was no illness.

"The job of the volunteer isn't to make a child better or cure their ailment," Kevin noted, letting each word leak out slowly and pronounced, as if he'd said the sentence before. "The purpose is to preserve one positive moment in time with them," he continued. "To create one memory of laughter and joy that may come back to them during a less fun time. That's what it is for me at least."

Kevin wasn't just reciting words from a work manual. He was clearly passionate about the organization, and I didn't doubt he'd had countless experiences with children in hospitals that I couldn't, at that time, possibly understand.

I decided to be open with Kevin about my concerns. I told him that I wanted to do anything I could to help, but that walking into a children's hospital would be a new and nerve-racking experience for me.

"It's natural to hear the phrase 'sick kids' and feel afraid." He smiled, obviously having heard my concerns before, maybe even having the same worries himself at one point. "Just remember, they're kids first and sick second. The examples I gave are not the common cases, thankfully. These are just kids with circumstances that are a little different than yours and mine."

I eventually told Kevin that I was in. I signed the necessary papers and collected a handful of pamphlets that better explained hospital protocol. Kevin told me that the organization worked with a number of hospitals around the city and that he'd get back to me later that week with the next available arts and crafts session. We parted ways.

Just like Kevin promised, I received an e-mail later that week. Since the organization's New York expansion was still fairly new, there was only one more general arts and crafts session left in the year. If I backed out I wouldn't get another shot any time soon. So, a few days after hearing back from Kevin I was off to New York University Langones Hospital for Joint Diseases Center for Children.

I made it to the hospital about twenty minutes early, feeling sick with nervousness. I paced outside for a few minutes in an attempt to gather myself. Kevin eventually spotted me and motioned for me to join him inside. He greeted me with a handshake and the energetic smile I remembered from our first meeting. Standing next to him was a good-looking blonde woman who couldn't have been much older than thirty.

"This is Clara, she'll be leading the activity today."

"I haven't seen you around before. First time?" she asked.

"Yes, first time. And I warn you, I'm not much of an artist."

Clara laughed, as if to reassure me it was an activity for kids, not a project I'd be graded on.

"Well, let's do this," she said, wasting no time and walking toward the front desk to sign in.

Kevin leaned in to tell me Clara was a renowned painter who had art shows all over the world.

"She's insanely humble, though," he added. "She never misses a chance to paint with the kids."

After signing in and receiving nametags, we made our way

into an elevator, accompanied by the nurse who'd be overseeing the hour-long arts and crafts session.

"The kids are so excited," the nurse said, as the elevator crept upward slower than any elevator I'd ever been in.

It left me with plenty of time to recap all the moments I'd been awkward around children. I've never been able to quite perfect my excited kid voice. If you heard me asking my six-year-old cousin how school was going, you'd think I was asking a college engineering student about his upcoming exams. Even when I've found myself in the situation of being the cool older guy playing video games with kids, I'm incapable of providing high-pitched words of encouragement. The most I'm able to mumble is, "How the hell did you just manage to kill me?" I've only ever held a few babies in my lifetime and was more petrified with each one. Worst of all, I don't even have a puppy voice. People don't trust anyone who doesn't go ape shit and hit Mariah Carey–style notes when a puppy prances into the room.

The elevator opened and we spilled out into a narrow hallway. The nurse led us to the bathrooms and instructed us to wash our hands before entering the room with the children. Inside the bathroom, I took my usual position in front of the mirror. Since arriving at the hospital, I couldn't help but feel frightened about what I might see. That's the terrible stigma surrounding illness: that it has to be something profound and visual for it to be real. Even though I wasn't sure what actually constituted a joint disease, I naturally imagined the worst. My mind, like most people's, has a tendency to lead me down some dark tunnels of thought when I have no choice but to assume. I suppose preparing for the worst is a natural reaction. Though I still felt guilty about the images I couldn't stop from running through my head.

We all met outside the bathroom and made our way to the main activity room together. Inside the room were eight small children ranging in age from about five to ten. Some were already huddled around a long plastic table, while others clung on to their parents who sat in chairs on each side of the room. There was nothing seemingly abnormal about any of the children. One girl was in a cast and another in a wheelchair. I also noticed a boy wearing what appeared to be a leg brace under his jeans, but my images of a quarantined-style room with tubes and beeping machines, not unlike that terrible scene in *E.T.*, were way off. It's refreshing when your unfounded assumptions are proven wrong, but at the same time you wish you had the sense to never have assumed in the first place.

As Clara introduced herself, I took my place at the end of the table and began distributing the equipment: tubes of paint, paintbrushes, cups of water, paper towels, and paint palettes. Clara was a natural. She had a remarkably soothing voice that instantly grabbed the attention of the kids.

I was caught off guard when she said the words, "This is Greg." Suddenly all eyes were on me.

"He'll be helping with the arts and crafts today. Say hi to Greg, everyone."

A collective "Hi, Greg" filled the room. I reciprocated with a half smile and stiff wave, unable to muster up the courage to even let them hear my voice. I could feel the awkwardness wash over me in a warm tingle, from my head downward. If I wasn't beaming red, I definitely felt like I was. I made sure not to lift my eyes to the side of the room where Kevin stood.

As Clara explained the basic mechanics of painting (small, steady strokes; cleaning the brush in water; mixing colors to make new colors), I turned to the small boy to my right, and using all the strength I had, whispered, "Are you ready to paint something cool?"

"Yeah," he whispered back, before throwing his hands up as if he'd just scored a goal.

I slipped him a high five under the table and felt both invigorated and redeemed, my heart racing from adrenaline.

Eventually Clara pulled out a stack of papers from her bag. Each piece of paper had an image of a Van Gogh self-portrait on it. It was one of many self-portraits Van Gogh painted in his lifetime, though the particular painting Clara chose pictures Van Gogh staring eagerly into the distance, his light blue suit and piercing eyes nearly identical to the backdrop of the oil canvas, his thick, red beard and slicked-back hair a stark contrast against the soothing blue.

"So do your best to make your painting look just like the one on the paper," Clara announced. "Now . . . go!"

The kids immediately grabbed for the proper colors and

smeared paint across the palettes. I grabbed some paint myself and worked on my own attempt at recreating the Van Gogh masterpiece. In between strokes I made sure to comment on the work of the young artists around me. With each newly uttered, "Wow, you're doing a great job," my words became more sincere and less forced. Kids would take turns coming up to me to distribute high fives and ask if I was a painter.

"No way," I'd tell them. "Look how much better your painting is turning out than mine."

Most of them would laugh and say, "Yeah, I know. Mine is really good!"

I felt more alive with each interaction. I thought about how much it had taken for me to be in the hospital, laughing and smiling with kids I'd been terrified of moments earlier.

I finished my painting and was surprisingly proud. Granted, my Van Gogh looked more like a sad Ryan Gosling in a dark blue suit, but I at least got the background right. I decided to take a lap around the room to clean up any of the unused brushes and palettes. As I made my way around the table I'd compliment each of the kids' paintings, which were, not surprisingly, just as good or better than mine. One of the boys tugged at my shirt as I walked by him and asked, "Hey, why are we painting you?"

The girl next to him chimed in: "Yeah, are you famous or something?"

Before long the entire table was in an uproar, demanding to know why they were painting pictures of me.

"You think I look like Van Gogh?" I asked.

They shouted back in unison, convinced the man on the paper was a painting of me. Clara and Kevin caught wind of the conversation and laughed.

Knowing I had to say something, I shouted, "Maybe that's my long lost brother," in a voice I didn't quite recognize. It was the most vocal I'd ever been around children, and it even had a high-pitched tinge. It felt different. It felt refreshing.

At the end of the hour-long session I said good-bye to Clara and Kevin.

"You did great," Kevin said.

"So funny that the kids thought you looked like Van Gogh." Clara laughed. "You know, I think I kind of see it, too. Something about the eyes."

Outside the hospital I was giddy with excitement. I hadn't done much, but it was more than I thought I was capable of. After all the assumptions and fears and bathroom pep talks, it was a success.

I reached for my phone and found a folded-up piece of paper in my pocket. It was one of the printed Van Gogh self-portraits I must have forgotten to throw out. I opened it and stared deeply into his blue eyes, looking for similarities and wondering what the kids saw in both him and me. He had red hair and a beard; I had brown hair and was clean-shaven. He was wearing a blazer and vest; I could barely tie my own tie. I decided to google the picture on my walk to the subway. I learned that Van Gogh painted the self-portrait in 1889, exactly one hundred years before I was born. Some art historians believed it might have been the last self-portrait he ever painted. Reading further into the history, I found that when Van Gogh first sent the painting to his brother, an art dealer, he attached a note that read, "You will need to study the picture for a time. I hope you will notice that my facial expressions have become much calmer, although my eyes have the same insecure look as before, or so it appears to me."

It made perfect sense. I was Van Gogh in the picture: a ball of insecurity hiding behind a seemingly calm face. It's funny how the kids could see that immediately. Insecurity, of course, can be so many different things. For me, it usually comes down to the understanding that I may not be doing something for the right reasons, like volunteering because I thought it would somehow protect me from the tragedies of life, and not because I actually wanted to give back in some way.

The second time around would be different, I told myself. I tell myself this a lot, but this time I really believed it, because thinking back about the kids I painted with, and all the others I didn't get a chance to paint with, it's clear that having a second chance is a luxury, not a guarantee.

Millennial Mousetrap

My first ever apartment was a small two-bedroom in Astoria, Queens, located directly above a deli with a neon sign and the kind of tuna salad you always think about ordering but never do. So I wasn't surprised when I saw a mouse. It was more of a shadow that darted past my feet one night while I staggered, half asleep, to the bathroom. It spurred a delayed shock in me— the mouse was probably back downstairs in the deli munching on crumbs by the time I flailed my limbs and jumped backward, like a lagging video-game character.

I was oddly proud that I had survived my first run-in with a New York City mouse. Growing up in suburban Long Island, the only things that ever got into my home were spiders and ants. I was in the big leagues now.

After I broke the news to my roommate Phil, who had grown up across the street from me, also without mice, we went on a search for the most classic-looking mousetrap on the market.

We decided on an old-school wooden trap with "kills mice" written across the package in large, no-nonsense letters. This was enough of a guarantee for us.

We set up one of the death traps with a dab of peanut butter as bait and placed it on top of the stove, where we had found mouse droppings. (For some reason, mice have the luxury of having their shit called droppings.) The next morning I woke to find a little gray body, cold and stiff, on the stove. The trap had come right down on its head, collapsing its skull in a gruesome way. I couldn't look at it for more than a few seconds at a time.

I felt conflicted about the small corpse in front of me. The mouse had seemed much more menacing when it was just a speeding shadow. Now he looked tiny and sad. Perhaps we could have compromised with it before going the murder route. Maybe the miniature shits were actually kind of cute. It was I who deserved to be branded with "kills mice," not the mouse-trap. I shook my head. Clearly, I was going soft.

Phil helped convince me that we'd made the right choice. Mice carried diseases. We couldn't spare the life of anything that took a dump where we cooked and ate. But I was glad I at least felt *some* remorse for my actions.

As we stood looking down at the mouse, like we were attending some miniature, horribly depressing funeral, I was reminded of a time when Phil and I were younger and came across a dead bird in the middle of the road where we were riding our bikes. We kept riding back and forth, our tires coming closer and closer to the body each time. Eventually one of us, I can't remember who, "accidentally" ran it over. The guts popped from the bird with force and we fled the scene as fast as our legs would pedal. The fact that I still feel sorry to this day has to count for something.

Over the next few months, mice would come and go. We'd find droppings in strange places or get startled by a quick-moving shadow with a tail. Each time we'd plop peanut butter onto a trap and within hours we'd be chucking a dead mouse into the trash. It was like clockwork. We woke up, went to our respective jobs, killed a mouse or two, and went to sleep. We ran a very efficient operation. At twenty-two years old, living on our own for the first time, we felt like we were handling the real world the way it was supposed to be handled. No questions asked.

But one day, we came home to find an untouched trap that was somehow missing its peanut butter. We stood above it, staring like it had a secret to share. Which it did. We determined that we had used too much peanut butter and the mouse was able to eat it without actually stepping on the trap. So we set up a new trap with a smaller amount and called it a day.

But for the next few weeks we'd wake up to the same untouched trap, perplexingly devoid of the peanut butter that had been added the night before. We did our research and learned that some mice are too light to set off a trap, even the classic wood and steel death machines we'd called on to carry out our dirty work. The next step up was a futuristic-looking mechanism that required the mouse to climb inside before snapping its deadly fangs shut, guaranteeing a kill each time. Compared to this sleek-looking robotic executioner, we may as well have been stoning the mice to death. Our mousetraps were straight out of *Tom and Jerry* and at least a decade behind modern mouse-killing technology.

We set the new trap up on the stove, which by then was caked in shit pretty much every morning. With the amount of free peanut butter we'd been offering the little guy it was no surprise he had to clean out his system so often. On top of the white stove, the shiny plastic trap looked like an alligator poking its long, crooked snout out of the water, waiting patiently to snatch its next meal. I went to bed confident.

The next morning we woke to find a long tail snaking its way out of the trap. Phil ran to look in excitement, but when he grabbed it the mouse jumped out and made a run for it. It made sure to stop on the counter and get a good look at us both, its beady eyes cutting right through us, before it took off under the stove. If it could have given us the finger, it would have.

From then on, the mouse terrorized our lives. Day in and day out it let us know it was faster than us, cleverer than us, and—through a series of inexplicably intricate maneuvers requiring splinter cell–like elusiveness—better than us. I have a theory now that a person isn't a true New Yorker unless they've encountered a mouse that has made them question the proposed hierarchy of species.

Every step we took in the apartment was a cautious one. We'd peek around corners and walk on tiptoes, our eyes darting to each corner of the room with every hint of movement. The place may as well have been haunted.

No matter how well we checked a room, the mouse would find a way to scurry past, scaring the living shit out of us each time. If we were on the couch watching a movie, it would run through our feet. If we had company over, it would do laps around the room, making sure every guest caught a glimpse. Each time I'd jump up in panic or let out a yelp more embarrassing and high-pitched than the last.

We were losing the battle in a psychological war. We were simply renting rooms in the mouse's apartment. Residents in a rodent house.

At the time, we had a third roommate, Ethan, living with us so Phil and I could cut costs by sharing one of the bedrooms. Ethan was the true definition of a stoner, unable to get through a day without being high. He went to work high, worked out high, ate high, lived high. His room was decorated with enough grinders, bongs, bowls, and rolling papers to start a wholesale business. Each day we'd ask him to not smoke in the apartment, and each day he'd give a heartfelt apology that truly convinced us he'd never do it again.

One night Phil and Ethan came back into the apartment after smoking. Whenever Ethan did go outside to smoke he'd invite Phil, as if to show off the fact that he was cooperating with our requests. We were all sitting on the couch, Phil and Ethan's mouse paranoia heightened since they were high, when we were startled by a loud scratching coming from the kitchen. The rapid scratches were relentless and sounded like nails quickly sliding across a chalkboard.

We made our way to the kitchen in slow motion, peeking our heads around the corner. Inside the sink was the mouse. The tiny bastard must have fallen in and couldn't quite make its way up the slick stainless-steel edges of the deep sink. It would get a running start each time, but its small body didn't have the momentum to carry it over the edge to freedom.

As afraid as we were to go near it, we understood this might be the only chance we'd get to end the nightmare. "We'll drop the trap on it," Phil suggested, and I realized he was right. The murder would have to be done with a trap. Anything else, like dropping a book or swinging a hammer, would be too real. The trap allowed you to at least sleep at night. The blood wasn't on your hands directly.

Phil picked up the cocked and loaded trap from the stove and held it steadily above the sink. The mouse sprinted from side to side in unpredictable zigzags. Phil dropped the trap, but the mouse easily eluded it. Phil tried this several times while anxiously giggling and dancing around on his tippy-toes as he reached in to retrieve it. After a few more tries it was obvious that the mouse was just too fast.

"If only we could slow him down somehow," Phil muttered.

Ethan's face lit up. "I have the greatest idea ever." Both their eyes were bloodshot and their slow speech hung in the air like the smell of gas. It occurred to me in that moment how high they really were.

"You know how weed, like, makes us slow and tired?" he asked. "What if, like, we got the mouse high to slow it down?"

A smile crept across Phil's face, as if the answer was that obvious all along. High conversations are often among the most poetic. They are profound in their simplicity and earnestness. A person in the midst of a high thought can never be thoroughly convinced that what they're saying isn't truth. There's something exceptionally admirable about that sincerity.

"This can work," Ethan said assuredly, desperate for us to believe him.

Ethan brought out his biggest bong and he and Phil took turns taking monster hits and directing the smoke into the sink with oven mitts. After about five hits each, the smoke was so dense in the sink you couldn't even see the mouse. Phil and Ethan could barely stand and were in the grips of the kind of howling, full-body laughter that can only be caused by a scheme devised with your friends. And weed.

After the smoke cleared and Phil and Ethan's coughing fits had settled down, we eagerly huddled together to take a look at the mouse. It stood still in one place, its beady eyes staring dead ahead.

"I think it's high," Phil whispered.

He was right. For the last few torturous months we'd only seen the mouse scurry feverishly around with endless energy, and now, after being on the receiving end of a few bong hits, he was as apathetic and stagnant as a regular pothead.

Phil raised the plastic trap over the little guy and this time it fell straight onto its target, swallowing the mouse up in one vicious snap. The problem was solved.

Ethan took another hit from the bong.

And people are worried about millennials running the world.

Confessions of a God-Fearing Atheist

If you were to ask me if I believe in God, I'd say it's hard to imagine there's one person overseeing this whole mess whose name isn't Mark Zuckerberg or who doesn't have top-level security clearance with the NSA. Yet some nights I find myself under my covers, apologizing to God in a half whisper for doubting His existence. Herein lies my dilemma with committing to one belief. I've met plenty of self-proclaimed atheists and a ton of people my age who wholeheartedly believe in God, though I find myself somewhere in the middle, prepared to live-tweet the second coming but not expecting it to ever actually happen.

I blame my uncertainty on the fact I grew up in an age where it takes two seconds and a Wi-Fi connection to find the answer to just about any question. Having instant accessibility to information makes it difficult to buy into the idea there's a power greater than the battery in our cell phones. It also makes it easy to dismiss religion as being outdated and man-made. When you type the phrase "Religion is" into Google's search bar, the autocomplete suggestions that appear are "bullshit," "dying," "the opium of the people," and "fake"—in that order. Of course, the one question the Internet can't answer is, What happens to us after we die? I mean what *really* happens. Not just the fact that worms eat through our decomposing corpses and fertilize the earth. Unless that is all that happens.

It's this fear of the unknown that leaves me hanging on to faith despite my skepticism. It's also why I end up apologizing to God more than I find myself praying. Aside from apologizing for doubting His existence, I'm often saying sorry for wondering things like, *Did Jesus ever get friend-zoned?* or *Will God ever be a trendy name for kids in Brooklyn?* Luckily, I was taught that God is willing to forgive anyone, which is an extraordinary deed. Even Santa keeps a naughty list.

When I do find the time to pray, my prayers are infrequent and selfish. I'll ask God to help me get a raise and make sure a store has sneakers in my size. Then I feel guilty and go right back to apologizing. The next day (especially if the sneakers were out of stock) I'm back to doubting there's anyone on the other end of the phone line of my internal thoughts. The cycle of confusion is a draining one.

When I was younger I attended Catholic mass on Sundays with my family, along with religious education classes once a week. Every Monday I'd file into the church basement with twenty other tireless kids to learn about Catholicism from a volunteer teacher who looked and spoke like he was in the mafia. I wasn't allowed to watch *The Sopranos* at the time, but from the scenes I'd caught my parents watching, I figured my teacher, with his slicked-back hair and larger-than-average gold cross around his neck, was a hired gun for God.

Religious education actually felt a lot like after-school detention, though that could have been the point. Throwing kids into a classroom in the church basement and giving them work that resembles what they receive in school is an effective method of teaching, after all. As far as I knew, Jesus was as real as George Washington, since they both had Xeroxed worksheets about their lives handed out by adults. So I made my communion and confirmation and ate the body and blood of Christ without giving it a second thought.

As I grew older I never denounced my faith. I sort of just stopped thinking about it, like a scab I'd finally learned to stop picking at. My mother on the other hand has always been religious. She's not fanatically religious and she doesn't push any of her beliefs on anyone else. But she does believe, and finds a great deal of comfort in the church and the community it offers. One day she was giving me a ride home to my apartment in Queens and played a CD of a priest's sermon in the car. I found it amazing how well I knew the passages, names, and songs from a childhood of attending church. It was like hearing the very first *Now That's What I Call Music!* album and realizing just how big of an impact those mainstream songs had on your life. But what did any of it really mean to me? Did the fact that I remembered prayers and the stories of some of the apostles mean I was religious? It reminded me of high-school science classes. Sure, I had memorized some facts for a few tests, but that didn't mean I really learned anything. If you were to ask me today what a sedimentary rock is, I'd probably say a type of music.

I decided then that I owed it to myself to form my own opinion about religion and faith as an adult. I figured the simplest way to do so would be to go back to church, and luckily there was one only a couple blocks from my apartment. The only problem was keeping the visits consistent. I'd go one week and walk out feeling surprisingly satisfied, though I couldn't tell if it was simply the same satisfaction that comes with checking something off a to-do list. Then I'd end up not going for a full month. I did attend a free weeknight showing of *Les Misérables* in the church's basement thinking it would make up for missing mass, but that just made me feel like I was cheating the system.

Since I couldn't manage to get to church frequently, I tried to at least keep my praying consistent. I knew plenty of people who believed in God but didn't affiliate with a particular religion. Maybe defining God on a personal level would be a more productive first step than jumping right back into a community of devout Catholics at least twice my age. With thousands of religions and traditions around the world, there's clearly no one right way to do things.

At night I made a conscious effort to not mention material things in my prayers. I instead asked God to look over the people I cared about most. After running through the list of names, I'd converse with Him briefly, the way I would with a distant uncle at a family reunion. I didn't say anything of much substance. I was really just trying to get acquainted and feel out the situation. Though on one particular night, I decided to lay it all out on the table and admit to Him that I was in the process of determining what I actually believed in. Then I thought, *if God were listening, wouldn't He just know everything I was thinking without my having to say it?* The idea made my head hurt the same way the ending of *Inception* did and I fell asleep shortly after.

When spring came around I planned a spiritual venture to Central Park by myself. I had read somewhere that to know God is to know nature and appreciate all that He has created. I may have seen it on a bumper sticker or refrigerator magnet. It was a gorgeous day and I strolled through the park alone, doing my best to take in my surroundings and keep an eye out for a sign. But mostly I just tripped over my own feet behind groups of tourists and running, screaming kids. I eventually settled on a bench in a less crowded area where I could do some quiet reflecting, but was distracted by a man having a picnic alone off to my right. I watched as he fumbled with a hot dog before it fell from his hands and into the dirt. Without hesitation he picked it up, wiped the specks of dirt and loose blades of grass off with his hand, and placed it back in the bun so he could continue eating. I decided I'd had enough nature for the day.

Praying and trying to find places of solitude in a bustling city soon became as sporadic as my church visits. During most weeks I was so consumed with work and my social life that I'd forget I was supposed to be on a makeshift spiritual journey. My life had become busier than it had ever been. The website I'd helped build from the ground up got acquired by a larger media conglomerate, things with my girlfriend were starting to get serious, and I had just landed my first book deal, which had been a dream since my first high-school English class. Things were going well, to say the least. And when things are going well, praying doesn't seem as necessary as when they're going to shit.

So, I was right back where I started, contemplating the existence of a higher power only if I'd had enough beers and the conversation with friends took that turn. It was nothing to be proud of, but it was how I'd been used to living my adult life. It was also how most of my peers were living their lives, so I didn't feel out of place. We're all so busy trying to leave our mark on the world in any way possible that we barely fit in time to call our parents and have relationships, let alone talk to a being that may not even be listening.

It wasn't until a few months after abandoning my lazy quest to find God that I was reminded of why I'd questioned my contradictory beliefs in the first place. I was taking my usual morning commute when, for whatever reason, I took extra notice of a woman handing out religious pamphlets. It's not at all rare to see people with tables set up on subway platforms in New York City, offering up free literature about faith and Jesus and everything in between. I had just never stopped to give them any thought.

This particular woman wasn't preaching the way I'd seen others preach about the power of the Lord in the dreary underground corridors of the subway. She simply stood there smiling next to her table with her arms folded, the way a teacher does when she's waiting for her class to quiet down. If she had a quota to fill, she wasn't doing a very good job. I decided to stop next to her table while I waited for the train. I tried to catch a glimpse of the pamphlets without her noticing my growing interest. The typed font mentioned something about finding eternal peace through God.

For the next couple of weeks, I eagerly made my way to the same spot on the subway platform each morning to find a place near the woman. Some days she was nowhere to be found, but on most days she was right there in her usual spot, under the busy corner of Fifty Ninth Street and Lexington Avenue. Whenever she was there, I stood near her, anticipating what she'd say if someone came over to her table. Though, nobody ever did, and so she just stood there smiling, waiting patiently for a taker.

In a way, I felt bad for her; but at the same time I admired her. I was desperate to know what made her so positive that her beliefs had value. What drove her to wake up each morning just to stand in the same spot, offering up a message that, it seemed, nobody was interested in receiving? Did she ever think she was wasting her time as she watched the world pass her by during morning rush hour? I envied her confidence.

One morning, I made a plan to pick up a pamphlet from her. At the very least it seemed like a nice gesture. I even woke up early to make sure I had enough time to miss a train or two if needed.

I never in a million years would have imagined myself approaching someone passing out religious paraphernalia in the subway, but that Monday morning when I arrived at the station platform, I immediately made my way to her table. I lingered for a bit before picking up one of the pamphlets.

"Hello," she said with a smile the moment my fingers gripped the paper.

"Hi," I replied.

"What is it you're looking for in God?" she asked in a gentle voice.

I was caught by complete surprise. I'd played out conversations with this woman in my head for days, but that straight-to-the-point question took me totally off guard. All I could do was stand there frozen as a list of possible responses ran through my mind.

Somehow, this woman had found a way to ask me the one question I hadn't asked myself. Throughout my entire ongoing quest for faith, I'd never stopped to consider what I'd actually hoped to find, or if I even wanted to find it. I suddenly felt like I'd gotten caught cheating on a test. Perhaps I was looking for assurance that there's an afterlife where I'd live happily ever after, a place in the clouds with a strong Wi-Fi connection. Who isn't curious about that? But that didn't feel quite right; isn't the point of having faith believing in something without ever needing definitive proof? Maybe I was simply nostalgic for the hymns and community that made up part of my childhood. It could have been that I just wanted something new to believe in.

Had I been forging a perpetual search for spirituality because it seemed like a better option than not searching at all? I didn't feel like I'd gotten any closer to discovering faith. I was still balancing on the fence between God's existence and His being entirely made up, ready to jump to either side if definitive proof were ever determined.

I noticed the light of an oncoming train creep around the edge of the platform. I looked back at the woman with a blank stare.

She smiled again, encouraging me to answer.

"Well," I started.

I paused again as the train hissed into the station in front of us. The crowd of commuters stepped closer to the platform's edge.

"Well . . . that's my train," I finally said. "Sorry," I added, before hurrying off, barely squeezing my way into the hot, crowded subway car before the doors closed.

As the train pulled away from the platform, I watched the woman's face, completely unchanged, disappear in a quick flash. Had she seen right through me?

It was clear I wouldn't be coming to a conclusion any time soon. If I wanted any peace of mind, I'd have to at least appreciate the fact I was asking questions. Even if my search was spurred on by selfish intentions, it was a start. A shitty start, but a start nonetheless. Luckily, God didn't create the universe in a day. Some things take time.

Maybe one day I'll find what I'm looking for, I thought. Maybe I wouldn't know what I was looking for until I stumbled upon it. Or maybe the search would go on forever. The only thing I knew for certain was that I'd be doing a lot of apologizing later that night, tucked under my covers, where I was safe and nobody asked questions.

Homeless Joe

Not many people can say they've played a part in making a homeless person famous. I can.

It all started when an Elite Daily writer, Dan, got writer's block, as all writers do. In an attempt to overcome the creative stagnation, an editor sent him outside to observe a homeless man on the corner of Twenty-Third Street and Park Avenue. Questions about this man, who held a cardboard sign that read "Seeking Human Kindne$$" and didn't look a day over twenty-seven, were beginning to float around the office. Nearly every morning he was on the same corner, sprawled out comfortably on the pavement with a small cup to collect spare change and dollar bills. And yet every morning he appeared to be in clean clothes, his hair strategically sculpted with styling gel. We couldn't help but wonder if he were really homeless and actually as young as he appeared. If he'd walked into the office for an interview I wouldn't have questioned a thing. I was even jealous of how effortlessly his hair fell into place, messy but calculated.

After a couple hours passed, Dan burst through the office door, nearly knocking over desks in excitement. "I've got a story!" he exclaimed. A few of us sat down in a conference room and Dan explained the time he'd just spent with the man he now identified as Homeless Joe. Between heavy breaths Dan told us that Joe was twenty-six and definitely homeless. The catch was, he wasn't technically homeless every night. According to Dan, Joe was a master of picking up women and convincing them to bring him back to their places. He'd use these one-night stands as a way to get some temporary shelter and take a shower. He'd even sneak in laundry when he could.

Joe told Dan he met most of these women in bars, where he'd spend his saved-up money on drinks. He claimed he was averaging 150 dollars a day, which, if true, would put him in an annual salary bracket significantly higher than the average millennial. And that income was tax free, the bastard. He also claimed he slept with three to four new women a week, which, from my experiences as a single male, would put him light-years ahead of the average (right??).

Dan was eager to spend as much time with Joe as possible. Joe had even hinted at being a fugitive on the run. He mentioned he hadn't seen his family, who lived in Boston, in years. He was apparently kicked out of college for selling drugs, though he was homeless by choice. From what Dan told us, Joe spoke of his situation as an expression of freedom. He viewed his circumstances as a way to prove you don't need to conform to societal norms to be happy.

The decision to let Dan further explore the story of Homeless Joe wasn't an easy one, mostly due to the fact that, at surface level, Joe deceived women and openly admitted to using drugs and drinking in public. It's not exactly the type of behavior that should be celebrated. On the other hand, Joe was an interesting case because he was so young and truly believed he was in control of his life. If he was making as much money and meeting as many women as he claimed, was he not, in a way, successful, even if by confused, self-absorbed standards? I know plenty of people who measure their self-worth by the same exact principles. They boast about how much casual sex they have and their high tolerance for Jägerbombs and warm Bud Lights. And yet Joe was doing all this without a job or home or any real structure in his life at all. Though behind the flashy smile, styled hair, and surprisingly suave pick-up lines, Joe was not a role model. What he was, however, was a reminder that life can take you places you never thought it would, based on the simplest decisions we make each day. Dan explained that Joe was once a good son and engaged student. He went to college and was a semester away from graduating. He was, for lack of a better term, a normal millennial. And though we hated to admit it, the story fascinated us all. We decided to give Dan the green light to pursue a piece on Joe, to, at the very least, see where the story would go.

It didn't take long to realize that a story on Joe, the not-so-average, clean-cut, womanizing, homeless-by-choice millennial, would be much more compelling with a visual component. It only took our video crew an hour with him on the street to determine he was a character the world would be interested in, for better or worse. Joe agreed, signed some papers, accepted some money for his time, and filming began immediately. So much for being a fugitive on the run, though the line of truth and exaggeration had been a blur from the start with Joe. To Joe's credit, his ability to pick up women was not an exaggeration. With cameras following him from a distance, he approached almost every woman that caught his eye, and even kissed a few of them right on the crowded street.

When the concise but action-packed short documentary hit the Internet early on a Monday morning, we weren't aware of the storm that would follow. The video starts out with Joe, as confident and laid-back as a retired billionaire, saying, "Since there's eight million people in this city, if you're not getting laid, you're an asshole." He goes on to refer to himself as a "cardboard all-star," and proudly announces, "I have no bad outfits." Joe then takes viewers through his daily routine, which consists of mixing cheap vodka with Gatorade, racking up wads of cash from strangers, and successfully picking up women all over the city. Perhaps Joe's most human moment comes toward the end of the documentary, when he admits, "The reason people give me the amount of money they do is because they realize that they're just that fucking close to becoming homeless." He then goes on to tell the youth of America to never end up like him. As the video wraps up, one is certainly left with an unfamiliar taste in their mouth, which was really the point of telling Joe's story in the first place. Simply put, Joe was a force unlike anything anyone had seen before, and the Internet responded in droves: some angry, some disgusted, and some unashamedly impressed by Joe's confidence and sense of self-worth, despite living on a street corner.

Within hours of Elite Daily's posting the video, the story was picked up by a number of publications, including *People*, *Cosmopolitan*, the Huffington Post, *New York* magazine, and Business Insider. Clips from the video even made it to a segment of the *Today* show. In the first day alone, the YouTube upload reached two million views, and would ultimately go on to reach over five and a half million. I even heard a couple debating about Joe's behavior on my train ride home from work that day. The man didn't see anything wrong with Joe's turning his shitty circumstances into a life he could at least somewhat enjoy. The woman was appalled. She believed everything Joe did was disrespectful and fueled by his own insecurities. *A day ago he was just another homeless person asking for money,* I thought.

The next morning, as I made my way from the train to the office, I noticed a long line of people gathered outside Pret a Manger on Twenty-Third and Park. I assumed they were offering free coffee or some other promotion. As I crossed the street toward the front of Pret, I could see Joe. He was standing in the middle of an excited crowd, holding a phone and snapping selfies. The line, it turned out, was to meet Joe, and it was nearly around the corner. He was officially an overnight celebrity. I watched as people passed by, taking notice of the line, then seeing Joe would exclaim, "Oh my God, it's that homeless guy from the video!" Then they'd either pull out their phones to snap a photo or get in line themselves. Joe was of course charging a small fee for each picture, and people were happy to give up their cash.

At some point throughout the day Joe even ditched his "Seeking Human Kindne$$" sign for a new one that read "Internet Sensation." Joe loved every minute of the attention, but there was a part of the whole ordeal that I couldn't quite wrap my head around. Joe's rise to notoriety was so rapid it almost seemed wrong. It was hard to imagine what Joe thought of the whole thing. Here was a guy who one day was spending money on drugs and sleeping on cardboard, and the next it appeared as if he were a household name. The biggest question that was beginning to form in my mind was, Is there a way to get Joe help, if he'd even accept?

My question was answered when Dr. Phil reached out to us. He wanted Joe to appear on his show so that he could convince him to go to rehab. We never knew the full extent of Joe's drug use, but he'd mentioned he'd been to rehab a handful of times.

As much as Joe enjoyed the spotlight, appearing on daytime TV to talk about his problems wasn't as appealing to him as charging for selfies on the street. It took some convincing, but a little over a month later there was Joe, sitting a few feet away from Dr. Phil on national television. He was dressed in a button-down shirt and blazer and his hair was as perfect as ever. Joe was all laughs, admitting to having drunk ten beers before the show. One of his eyes was so bloodshot it was difficult to look at. Dr. Phil on the other hand was his usual all-business self, not enthused for a moment by Joe's carefree attitude. For most of the show it was like watching a heavyweight title bout. Joe's laid-back egotism was for the first time being matched by Dr. Phil's searing inquisitions. When he looked Joe directly in his red eyes and asked, "What are you running from?" the audience provided a barrage of "oohhs" and "aahhs." A handful of us watched from the office, shaking our heads in disbelief at what we'd caused.

Dr. Phil finally broke Joe as much as Joe could ever be broken. A new side of the cardboard Casanova had emerged as the two spoke about how Joe wakes up shaking and victimizes those around him. It was an honesty we hadn't been able to see behind Joe's hardened exterior. Even the warnings Joe had given us seemed feigned, as if to say, "Only I am fit to succeed at this lifestyle." But now nothing seemed phony as he admitted that every day he was running from reality.

Joe eventually agreed to give rehab a shot. Only time would tell whether it would pay off or not, but at the end of the day,

Dr. Phil did what he'd set out to do. He had taken our Internet sensation and brought him back down to reality. As quickly as Joe had gone from drug addict homeless guy to quasi celebrity, he'd been brought back down to earth by America's favorite TV-ready psychologist.

Such is the cycle of instant fame, I suppose. Far gone are the times it took years of training and networking to build up a name for yourself. Fame was once a by-product of hard work and dedication toward a craft. It was an industry thing, more or less. But fame in this day and age is fleeting and fast. It's not all about talent and paying dues. It's about getting yourself in front of people's eyes, and since our eyes are pretty much extensions of our phone and computer screens, it's not as hard as it once was. Joe, who experienced his moment of fame just for living an unconventional and pretty illegal life (besides the drugs he admitted to stealing hair gel from Walgreens every morning), is an example of just how much sense the viral nature of today's nontraditional celebrities makes. (That is, not much.) Though, his instant rise in the public eye is what eventually put him on the road to rehab, so there is a glimmering hope somewhere in the mess.

For most of us, we tend to fantasize about fame and notoriety at least once in a while. We don't necessarily all try to attain it, but it doesn't stop us from pretending our shower or car is a ten-thousand-person arena as we belt out tunes. The desire for our names and faces to be known is natural, and if it's not, living in an age where a homeless person can end up signing autographs is causing it to become natural.

Savior of None

When I arrived in Brazil for the 2014 World Cup I expected to see flags lining the streets and parties on every corner. I'd imagined Italians dancing with Swedes; Brazilians raising glasses with Germans; the British scoffing at the French before hugging it out. Unfortunately, there were no such celebrations. In fact, there was hardly anyone on the streets at all. I couldn't for the life of me figure out why a city hosting the largest single-sport event in the world, in a country where soccer is religion, would be so deserted.

It turns out celebrations were happening, only they were happening in Rio de Janeiro, São Paulo, and the other vibrant host cities teeming with global visitors and enthusiastic locals. They definitely weren't happening where I was, in Brasilia, the country's capital and perhaps the stalest city in all of South America.

Brasilia is a planned city, which means the country decided one day to build it from scratch, like a child playing with Legos.

The expansive piece of land in the middle of the country was their playroom, and they came up with a quaint yet sprawling metropolis that is, for some reason, shaped to look like an airplane from above. Once the city was finished being built in 1960, it became Brazil's official capital, replacing Rio de Janeiro, which has, to its credit, remained the capital of beautiful women and beaches.

What Brasilia did have to offer was a newly renovated soccer stadium just in time for the World Cup, and my travel partner Kyle and I had tickets to two games there. We'd have to sacrifice the beachside festivities of Rio, but as they say, it's all for the love of the sport. This decision is not surprising when you consider that when we attended the 2010 World Cup in South Africa, we decided we'd see more games if we stayed in Johannesburg, a veritable murder and crime capital, rather than Cape Town, one of the most beautiful destinations in the world.

Even the hotel concierge had a difficult time suggesting what we do in Brasilia. The only real options for two twenty-four-year-olds were a mall directly across the street from the hotel and a small strip of bars along a lake called Lago Sul. The few restaurants worth trying in the city were out of the question since they'd already been booked for the week. Some people had at least done their research.

After only one day we realized the mall had nothing to offer and Lago Sul's bar scene was anemic. There's also something borderline insulting about looking out onto a lake when you had visions of a clear blue ocean.

On our second night we decided to stay in the hotel room. Watching Brazilian television shows we didn't understand and drinking all the beer in the minifridge seemed like a more worthwhile option than going out just to be disappointed.

At about midnight, after already restocking on cans of the local beer, I stepped onto the room's balcony to escape the blaring Portuguese commentary coming from the TV. Our third-floor room overlooked a sketchy, dark side road, and down below was a group of three women, each one in skirts shorter and heels higher than the next. I watched as cars crept down the street and the girls perked up, taking slow, delicate strides toward the road as if walking a runway.

I stood motionless, afraid of being spotted, and whispered into the room: "Kyle, I think there are prostitutes outside our window."

The only experience I'd ever had with a prostitute was back in New York. A friend of mine, Jay, was visiting from California and decided to make a late-night call to a number he'd found online. The website promised "quality female companions for all occasions." I was on my couch with my roommate Phil when Jay walked in with Destiny and introduced her like a last-minute prom date.

Destiny looked us up and down and said, "Y'all aren't those crazy kind of white boys are you?"

We shook our heads no.

"You guys interested in a gangbang?" she asked.

It was the first time anyone had ever pegged me as someone willing to participate in a gangbang. The thought had never crossed my mind, but suddenly I felt like a different person. The next day I had the urge to tell everyone I came in contact with. It took everything in me not to lean over to the Starbucks barista and say, "Hey, I'm not sure if you know this about me, but I turned down a gangbang last night. I could have done it if I wanted to."

The Brazilian prostitutes were different, though. They were doing all the stereotypical, street-corner things you'd expect a prostitute to do. They were either really good at their jobs or watched a lot of movies.

Eventually a pickup truck pulled over and one of the girls made her way to it. She leaned her entire upper body through the passenger-side window. I called for Kyle, this time in a voice he'd hear over the television: "There are definitely prostitutes outside our window."

We spent the next thirty minutes studying the girls' every move from the balcony. They'd wave to cars and accentuate their backsides by leaning slightly to one side. Some cars would only honk and flash their lights as they drove by, but at least one would pull over to talk every five minutes or so.

"Why haven't the cops come yet?" Kyle asked. A quick Google search revealed that street prostitution was perfectly legal in Brazil, and it turned out that Brasilia was the place to go if you were looking for a good time. The hotel district, where we were staying, apparently had some of the best hookers in the country. No wonder no one was spending money on drinks at the lake or shopping at the mall.

"These are the best of the best," I told Kyle.

"Yup. I can tell."

A half hour quickly turned into an hour. There was something mesmerizing about watching the girls go about their business. They'd each take turns approaching cars, and when traffic died down they'd run to a nearby tree and take quick swigs from a liquor bottle they'd stashed. What confused me was that nobody had struck a deal yet. Every car seemed to decide against going through with the deed at the very last minute, and the girl whose turn it was would walk back to the group increasingly disappointed.

Kyle and I started taking bets on which girl would get picked up first and what kind of car Prince Charming would roll up in. Each time a new car pulled up we'd get giddy with suspense, like kids that had just found a peephole into the girls' locker room. Though, as more cars came and went, leaving the girls alone on the corner, I couldn't help but feel bad.

We'd been watching them so long I'd begun to create backstories in my head that I started to believe. The shortest one with the red miniskirt and black halter top worked as a waitress in a cafe during the day, but it wasn't covering the expenses for her sick mother. The tall one with the fishnet stockings was one semester away from finishing school, and her close friend, the girl carrying the big purse, was trying the whole prostitution thing out for the first time ever. She figured it'd beat the wages she was making across the street at the mall.

"I have to go down there," I said to Kyle. "I have to meet them."

"There's no way I'm going down there," he replied.

It took a full fifteen minutes and another beer each before Kyle agreed to take the walk with me. I could see it in his eyes—he was just as curious about these girls as I was.

Once outside, we regrouped on the side of the building. I had no clue what I was going to say, but I knew I wouldn't be satisfied until I saw the girls up close.

"We're just going to say hi," I instructed. "Just a friendly hello." Kyle followed my lead.

The girl in the red miniskirt, the one with the sick mother and the job at the cafe, was closest to us. As we walked toward her she immediately shifted her stance and puckered her lips. She was a cute girl, no older than twenty-five. She had long dark hair and wide, bright eyes. It was hard to believe that after all the cars that had stopped at the corner not one guy had picked her up.

"Hi, I'm American," I said once I reached her. It was the first thing that came to mind.

"Sexo for two?" she immediately asked, nodding toward Kyle, who was standing behind me.

"No sexo," I responded. "What's your name? I'm Greg."

"Sexo for one?"

"No sexo for anyone. We just wanted to say hello. This is our first time in Brazil."

Her eyes grew even wider and I could tell the other girls were talking about us.

"Just hello," I continued. "Friends. No sexo. Just talk." Her face was blank.

Desperate for her to understand my friendly intentions, I pulled out my phone and held it out in front of us. "Selfie?" I asked. She gave out a loud yelp and ran back to her friends while mumbling, "No, no, no, no."

"I think it's time to go," Kyle muttered.

Back upstairs I watched as she waved down a car. After a few minutes of talking through the window she opened the passenger door and climbed in.

"She got in a car," I yelled to Kyle, but within seconds she was back outside with her arms folded.

"False alarm," I corrected myself. "She can't catch a break."

The next afternoon we attended our first game of the World Cup, an exciting match between France and Nigeria. Suddenly there were other people in the city. I had no idea where they'd come from, but they packed into the stadium with a capacity of over sixty-five thousand. Based on their songs and endless chants, I gathered they were local Brazilians rooting for a Nigerian upset.

Once the game was over and France claimed the victory, the crowd quickly dispersed, and the city flatlined. The few excited

French fans wandered aimlessly, unsure where to celebrate. The even fewer Nigerians did the same, with no clue where to sulk. Kyle and I did the only thing there was to do and headed toward the mall.

"There's really something about those prostitutes I can't get out of my head," I admitted. "That one was so robotic. Sexo and nothing else."

"Sexo pays the bills," Kyle concluded before we made the same rounds through the mall as we had the previous day.

Back in the hotel room that night I found myself once again perched on the balcony, eager to see if the girls would return. At around ten they appeared and took their positions. Since it was earlier in the night they had to catwalk their way around the occasional tourists and families with children that strolled down the sidewalk.

Kyle and I spent the next couple of hours watching the girls below and clearing out the restocked minifridge. Our next game was in four days. That meant four more days in Brasilia, drinking minifridge beer and spending more time in the same mall than the zombies from *Dawn of the Dead*.

"We need to make friends or something," Kyle announced.

"They're right down there," I replied, excitedly pointing at the girls on the street. "That's what I've been trying to say. They're dying to be saved. You know how boring it must be standing on the same sidewalk?" I jumped up on the balcony railing and extended my arms, mimicking Christ the Redeemer, the iconic statue of Jesus that overlooks Rio, to the best of my wobbly ability.

It took more than one beer to convince Kyle to take the trip downstairs with me again, but this time I had a plan. The idea was to offer the girl who denied my hello the previous night money to take a break. There'd be no sex. She could just translate the TV shows for us and have a beer. Anything that even for a short hour didn't require her to flaunt her body to passing drivers on a dark side street. I had some money to spend anyway, considering we weren't going out at all.

As I approached her on the street she tensed up and began mumbling "no."

"No pictures," I promised. "I have money. Money for you."

She walked over to give me a chance. "American money?" she muttered in a thick accent. I'd read reports before we traveled that free English classes were being offered to Brazilian prostitutes ahead of the World Cup.

"How much money for you to come upstairs with no sexo?" I made sure to add extra emphasis to the "no."

"We can watch TV and drink beer. Just for one hour," I added. "I pay you for no sexo."

"Only money for sexo," she replied. "Sexo only."

I was shocked. If someone asked me my price to take an hour off work to drink beer and watch TV, I'm pretty sure I'd be able to come up with an answer on the spot: yes. And my price probably wouldn't be all that much. In fact, I'd pay for the opportunity.

"Look," I said, in a less playful tone. "I want to save you from the sidewalk. Just for an hour. Take a break from this. I will pay you."

"Sexo," she replied in a stern tone. For the first time she stopped fidgeting and looked me in the eyes. "No save me," she said, her words precise and cutting. She turned and joined the two other girls and the three of them walked around the corner and out of sight.

Kyle and I looked at each other, speechless.

"Well, you scared them away," he finally said. "I think it's time to go again."

Before going to bed that night I made one last trip out to the balcony. The girls were back, but the tallest one, the girl with one semester left, wasn't there. They leaned against the tree where they'd previously stashed the bottle. The gentle warm breeze caused the leaves above them to shake ever so slightly. I would have given anything to know what they were thinking, and why my offer seemed to offend them so much. Rejection is never easy to understand.

The next day Kyle and I opened our first beers earlier than we had the other days. "About twelve hours till the show starts," Kyle joked, referring to the prostitutes' nightly appearance.

"Check flights to Rio," I replied. Kyle laughed at the idea. "I'm serious, check flights to Rio. We're not staying here another night." Once Kyle realized I was serious we were like crazed stockbrokers when the trading floor opens. We opened our phones and laptops and ran around the room like madmen spewing out times and screaming prices. We'd be able to stay in Rio for the next two days before our game back in Brasilia if we could find the right flights and a place to stay.

"I found a reasonable round-trip!" Kyle finally shouted, after digging through every travel site the spotty hotel Wi-Fi would connect to.

"Flight leaves in two hours. We book it now or it's another lonely night on the balcony."

We made it to the airport with only a few minutes to spare and boarded the plane drenched in sweat and disheveled.

When we finally touched down in Rio it was as if we'd been freed from prison after serving time for a crime we didn't commit. It was difficult not to drop down and kiss the ground. After leaving our bags in the shared apartment we'd booked in the airport five minutes before our flight, we headed to the beach.

It was nighttime, but the streets were buzzing with a dazzling mix of languages, all merging into one extravagant hum. Colombians played drums and danced. Americans chugged beers at small bars built on the sidewalk. Japanese women took pictures with local Brazilians. The trip we'd imagined in our heads was finally real.

As we strolled along the edge of Copacabana beach, Christ the Redeemer eventually came into sight, perched high on top of a mountain overlooking the entire city below. Colorful lights illuminated its enormous body, which looked as if it were float-ing unattached in the night sky.

"We're the prostitutes now," I joked with Kyle, pointing up at the statue.

We laughed, but I couldn't quite shake the feeling that I was being watched as we continued along the beach. Looking back up at the statue with its outstretched arms and chiseled features, it was hard to tell if it was asking our permission to save us or simply judging. Maybe I'd know the difference one day.

The Spaces We Share

A few weeks ago I found myself staring at pictures of two identical-looking gray couches for nearly an hour. I swiped back and forth between photos until my thumb was raw and eyes strained. I couldn't, for the life of me, see a difference between them, except that one was from Target and the other from Wal-Mart. I put my phone down and took a long hard look at the couch I currently own. It's a beat-up-looking brown leather hand-me-down. It has character in its creases and personality in its stains, and best of all it was given to my roommate and me for free. The new, sleek-looking gray couches were around six hundred dollars each, not including shipping. I didn't know Wal-Mart or Target sold things for six hundred dollars. After finally picking one—the couch from Target, I think, because it had a cooler-looking pillow in the photo—I texted my decision to my girlfriend Brittany. She immediately texted back, "Yay!" Followed by, "It feels so official that we're moving in together."

For the first time since we'd discussed living together months back, it did feel official. It's not that I even had much of an opinion about which couch we got, but reading the descriptions about durable polyester and wooden frames with a handsome espresso finish felt like reading an obituary about the first twenty-five years of my life. I was in mourning for myself.

When my father was my age, he was already married. My mother was four years younger at twenty-one. Times have changed of course. Couples are taking more time before getting married and making babies, and I'm certainly in that boat. But to think of my father married at twenty-five, preparing to buy a home and bring a child into the world, I feel slightly pathetic about the uneasiness I have about moving in with a girl for the first time.

After two years of dating, Brittany started asking when we'd take the leap and live together.

"I really don't want to give up my place and I don't think Phil is going to move out," I'd tell her.

My apartment was a great find. It's over a thousand square feet and the ceilings are about ten feet high. There's even a clear view of the Manhattan skyline from my bedroom window. I don't know how I got so lucky, but in New York City, you don't question these things. You just thank the universe and try to be nice to at least one person a day. The apartment is a one-bedroom, but since it's so big, Phil and I had a temporary wall installed to convert it to a two-bedroom. It was difficult for Brittany to argue with my concern over losing such a nice place.

Then one day Phil asked if we could talk. He sat me down and said, "I'm going to move in with Arianna once the lease is up." Arianna was his girlfriend of about a year.

"How are you so sure?" I asked, slightly panicked.

"I'm there all the time anyway," he responded. "I'd rather give it a try sooner than later."

He was at her place every day and slept there every night. I'd basically been living alone in the apartment for the past six months with more space than I knew what to do with.

"I guess you're right," I told him. "In that case, I think Brittany may move in."

"Why do you say it like that?" he asked.

"Like what?"

"Like you're scared."

"Because I am."

I've had some memorable milestones in my life. I graduated college. I landed a dream job. I helped build Elite Daily to the point it got sold. I got a book deal. I watched my brother get into college and my parents turn fifty. Yet none of those events had ever made me stop and consider just how quickly life goes by. That only happened the moment Phil's name was taken off the lease and Brittany began moving her things in. That was the first time in my life I could feel time tapping me on the shoulder and breathing down my neck. It could be because life is often measured by just a few landmark moments. If you think of the generic course of someone's life, they grow up, get married, have kids, become grandparents, and die. Hopefully peacefully. Probably from cancer.

When I received the e-mail from Brittany with the links to the two couches, everything slowed down. I suddenly saw myself the way I see my parents, as veterans in the game of life, moving forward against their will like pieces to a board game. They say one day you blink and you're fifty years old. I'd blinked and I was twenty-five, halfway there. Where would I be after my next blink? And the one after that? How many couches will I have owned by then?

The panic, of course, had nothing to do with Brittany, so I did everything in my power to hide my discomfort.

"I'm nervous," I'd tell her. "But a good nervous."

A part of me was excited to take the next step in our relationship, while the other part stared intently into the distance, watching my youth fade away in the foggy night like Gatsby's cherished green light.

I remember the day we both told our parents we'd decided to live together. My father and her mother approved immediately. My mother and her father took a little more convincing. They are both progressive and modern people, but they still held on to the ideal that you shouldn't live with someone until you're married. This, of course, is far from the general sentiment people have today. Things were different in the eighties when couples got married after high school and people still carried cash in their wallets. One night at dinner my brother and I both explained to our mother that we'd never feel comfortable marrying someone without knowing if we could tolerate living with that person first. Maybe divorce rates wouldn't be as high as they are if more people did the same back in the day.

Her response was, "So you're just going to live with every girlfriend you end up having to see if you can tolerate them?"

Almost simultaneously, Cole and I said we'd never move in with someone unless we thought there was potential to marry them. Those words played back in my head over and over as the move-in date with Brittany inched closer.

The first time it became difficult to hide my angst was when Brittany planned a trip to HomeGoods. HomeGoods is a home furnishing and decor store that smells like balsa wood and has a checkout line that is somehow always the same length, no matter what time of day you go. I'd been to the store plenty of times before, but always as an antsy child following my mother around while she spent way too much money on picture frames and linens. The store was packed from wall to wall with an assortment of trinkets and furniture that had no meaning or purpose in my life at the time. For all I knew, it could have been a well-organized garbage dump.

Entering the store as an actual customer with a purpose and near-empty apartment ready to be furnished made me dizzy. *How'd I end up at this point so quickly,* I wondered as the automatic doors slid apart and a sea of affordable clutter hit me squarely in the face.

The days of hand-me-down furniture would soon be over. Dorm-room chic a thing of the past. The adult responsibility of living with another person who's not just a come-and-go room-mate requires an adult aesthetic. This means spending money on things you'd never thought to spend money on before. Things like soap dispensers and towel racks. Walking through HomeGoods with Brittany was overwhelming, not just because of the variety of items, but also because it occurred to me I'd never given any thought to how I'd want my home to look. My apartment as it stood didn't even have artwork. I have a nice TV that was a gift from an ex-girlfriend, but besides that my couch, dinner table, TV stand, and chairs are all hand-me-downs. My apartment before that one was decorated with things I stole off the street: traffic cones, a cardboard cutout of the lottery guy, and floral-pattern chairs I'm pretty sure gave me bed bugs. I'd never considered the apartments I'd lived in to be homes. Home was always my parents' house, where I grew up.

Ditching the roommate lifestyle to live with a serious girl-friend meant establishing some sort of a home, or at the very least forging a level of comfort and warmth. Imagining a dream home is easy, but having to choose actual things among the sprawl of price tags and handmade bookends shaped like owls is a bit more difficult.

I followed Brittany through the store as if a string attached me to her. I felt like a lost dog following around the first person that pet me and asked where my owner was. She seemed so comfortable browsing, and I looked like I'd forgotten to study for a big math test. I observed everyone else in the store. Most of the shoppers were couples. The others were women who were by themselves, perusing the aisles the way people did when video-rental stores were still around.

The men in the relationships were clearly more seasoned than I was. They still trailed behind their wives, but they were at least prepared to give their opinion on whatever item was picked up and waved in front of them. Any time Brittany pointed something out I froze, unsure if the particular item were something I'd want to see every day of my life. It's funny how once you commit to something big like moving in with a girlfriend, there's an endless series of smaller commitments that follow. A couch is a commitment. Deciding which side of the bed to sleep on is a commitment. These commitments seem small on their own, but all the commitments together eventually make up your environment, your routine, your life. I'd see a coffee table I liked, but then I'd wonder if I'd like it two years down the road and doubt whether or not I ever liked it in the first place.

Brittany eventually spotted a yellow throw blanket and said it would be a perfect accent color to complement the gray couch. I didn't disagree that it would pair nicely with the couch, but I was afraid one firm "yes" would open the floodgates, and I'd end up knee-deep in furniture and accessories I wasn't positive I liked. The same way that first sip of alcohol can lead to a long night out after you've promised yourself you'd stay in and get some sleep, or how that one bite of bread at a restaurant leads to eating half a loaf after you'd convinced yourself you'd stay away from carbs.

Brittany could sense my apprehension. "Let's just walk around with it and see how we feel before we check out," she said.

Then, only moments later, she turned with the blanket held closely to her face and said with puppy eyes, "It's like it's already part of the family."

"Let's just get it," I replied. I was fine being the confused guy, but nobody wants to be the bad guy.

By the end of our attempted shopping spree we didn't have much in our cart. There was the yellow blanket and a shower mat. The last item we were deciding on was a piece that could apparently be used to store extra towels and toilet paper. I'm not exactly sure what to call it. It's one of those miscellaneous home-decor purchases that you can only really refer to as a *piece*. The type of hard-to-define furniture that prompts people to say things like, "Wow, I love that piece near your bathroom. Great find!" Or, "That piece you picked up is to die for. It really makes the apartment come alive."

If I had to describe it, it's about the height of a nightstand with a small glass door on the front. It's wooden and is painted an off-white color. It has the general qualities of an antique, but with a hundred-dollar price tag it's obviously not. Brittany liked the idea of placing it at the end of my hallway, catty-cornered near the bathroom door. I agreed the piece was nice as far as pieces go. Though it was difficult to envision spending money on something with such little function. We eventually decided it was the adult thing to do, so we threw it in our cart and brought it to the register.

With only a couple weeks until Brittany moved in, she asked if I could bring the piece back to my place. For some reason this struck me as a strange request. Logically, it made the most sense. The piece, after all, was purchased for my place, where Brittany would soon be living, so why wouldn't I bring it back with me? Yet, I didn't feel quite ready to be left alone with it. I was overcome with the same concern I've felt when holding a baby and the mother walks away.

Back at my apartment I placed the piece in the corner near the bathroom. Sometimes all it takes to completely change the feel of a place you were once familiar with is filling up a small space. It wasn't a good or a bad change. It was just different. A space that was once available was now occupied. It's fascinating how much ownership you can feel over nothingness. Space (especially in New York) is hard to come by. It's expensive and always in demand. I've always been extra protective of my space. I have a difficult time sharing a bed or having someone sit too close to me while I work. Sharing isn't something we're born understanding. It's a lesson we all have to learn as children. And even as adults, it's something that has to be learned over and over again. Sharing material things is the first step, but sharing the personal space we feel is ours requires a lot more selflessness.

The first night after putting the piece in the hallway I woke up at around two in the morning and stumbled half asleep to the bathroom. Catching a glimpse of the piece's shape in the corner of my half-opened eyes made my body spasm in fear. It might as well have been an intruder standing in the corner, not as concealed by the darkness as they thought. This happened the following night as well, and I nearly tore an ACL from jumping out of my skin. By the third night I had yet to get used to the newly filled space casting an unfamiliar shadow and was startled once more while walking to the bathroom.

"Damn you!" I yelled. "Stop scaring me."

By the fourth night, seeing the piece in the once empty hallway didn't cause me to physically throw my body in fear anymore. Instead it evoked more of a quick gasp and momentary flutter in my stomach. In the morning I took a long hard look at the piece in all its strangeness. I noticed the price tag was still hanging from the small knob on its front. It could have been a sign to return it, but I decided to find a scissor and remove the tag. *You might as well make yourself comfortable*, I thought while crouched down in front of it, face to face for the first time.

When the fifth night came around it didn't surprise me at all when I made my way from the bedroom to the bathroom. (If anything, I realized how consistently I'd been getting up to pee in the middle of the night.) This time I nodded to the piece as I passed, letting it know it didn't surprise me.

As I write this, I'm counting down the days until Brittany officially moves in, and I know the piece will still take some getting used to, though it is slowly but surely becoming part of the apartment. Dust has even begun to settle on its smooth surface and on the floor underneath it. I haven't cleaned it yet. I want it to get a bit dustier and used before even newer pieces start taking up the space around it. By then I imagine it will feel like an old friend. Fast-forwarding in my mind I know it's just one small piece in what will be a collection of a lot more pieces. Soon enough there will be nightstands and coffee tables and curtains. The couch has been ordered. I can even picture candles lighting up each room. By themselves all these things are strangers in a new place, but together they will amount to something I can call my home. Or better yet, our home. Because what good is all this space if it can't be shared?

Life on the Other Side of the Internet

Riding the subway to work one day, I noticed the girl next to me scrolling through an article on her phone and laughing to herself. I could easily see from the large logo on the top of her screen that it was from Elite Daily. It was titled "26 Struggles of Having Boobs That Aren't Big, but Aren't Tiny Either," and was an article I recognized quickly because, whether I'd like to admit it or not, it was my idea.

Noticing my gaze, she turned and looked at me, so I flashed my Elite Daily bracelet, like an off-duty cop who just happened to walk into a bank, midrobbery.

"Are you a fan of the site?" I quickly asked.

"Yeah." She smiled, excited by the coincidence. "I love how it feels like the articles are written specifically for me."

I did everything in my power not to look down at her chest.

Then she asked me the question most people ask: "Do you actually, like, know what people want to read?" Usually people will ask this in a condescending manner, as if they're on the verge of making me reveal something. Sometimes they'll even throw in a wink or a slight nod, hoping I'll respond with something like, "Nope, it's all one big game of throwing shit against a wall until it sticks."

"The short answer is no," I responded. "But the slightly longer answer is yes."

She nodded, obviously confused by my attempt at a joke.

"That article you're reading was my idea though," I added.

She flashed a hesitant smile. I could tell she was thrown off by the idea that I, the stranger with the penis and the testosterone and the scattered stubble not quite connecting into a beard, could be the brains behind an article about boobs that seemed to so perfectly match the description of her own. Granted, I didn't write the article. I'm not even sure why I thought of it in the first place. But I did assign it to a much more qualified writer of the female persuasion. Needless to say, the two of us kept to ourselves for the remainder of the train ride.

Similar occurrences happen more often than I'd ever expect. Luckily, they're not all as awkward. Usually people will notice my Elite Daily bracelet or T-shirt and ask to take selfies, because yes, being associated with a popular website warrants celebrity status on the New York City subway. Others will notice and shoot me a look I know translates to, *I fucking hate you. I see you all over my social media like a case of herpes I can't get rid of.* These polar-opposite reactions are the inevitable by-product of working online, which is a strange place if you haven't already figured that out for yourself. I've noticed the same thing happen to a girl I see every so often on the train wearing a Buzzfeed shirt. She'll either be greeted with enthusiastic high fives or venomous stares. Users of the Internet are either uproarious in their applause or ruthless in their judgment, and apparently even in real life.

People have favorite websites or blogs because they love the fact there are places where strangers can fearlessly say the same things they're thinking but may have never said out loud. At the same time, people despise websites for allowing strangers to say things they may not agree with. Of course, everyone is entitled to his or her own opinion. The job of a successful website is to start conversations. And also to be all over social media like a case of herpes people can't get rid of.

The odd beauty of the modern-day, millennial-focused website is that it often feels like an honest, intelligent, outgoing friend, who sometimes gets too drunk on weekdays but who can explain to you what's going on in Syria and rant about the building effects of global warming. And you can't always agree with your friends.

On a larger scale, this is also the beauty of the Internet. For most people, the Internet is both a source of daily procrastination and a perpetual stream of knowledge. Logging on to a website, getting lost in a Google search, or scrolling through a social-media page can be a much-needed break from a terrible day job as much as it's an instant pathway to all the information a person needs to at least somewhat understand the world they're living in.

People tend to wake up, wipe the tired from their eyes, and immediately plug into their phones or laptops to consume the day's happenings, considering information, opinions, and advice from people they'll most likely never meet in real life. There's usually no question as to where all the stories come from and what goes on behind the scenes to make them appear at one's fingertips almost effortlessly. But why question something that's there for the taking? Like food samples at a supermarket or lollipops at a doctor's office.

Once I began working for Elite Daily, subsequently becoming one of "those people you'll probably never meet in real life," the people who did know me in real life became increasingly curious about what working for something that seemingly only exists when they power on their computers and phones could possibly be like.

"There's no secret Internet laboratory," I'll tell people. "We're still just people in an office building. There aren't wires running from our brains to some database." Most people find this hard to believe. One time I added, "Movie sets aren't as glamorous as the final product either," and it seemed to have helped.

After convincing people that my coworkers and I get up for work the same way everyone else does each day, it's usually then a matter of convincing them that my day is not one big party.

I get that misunderstanding—the average age in my office is twenty-five and the founder started the company when he was twenty-one. It's hard to believe, I know, but despite the rampant ADHD and alleged "entitled nature" attached to us millennials by traditional media, we do know how to get work done. (In some ways, better than most, actually.) It did take close to a year to convince my parents and friends that my job was legitimate and had a promising future, though. It's not that easy when your professional jargon actually consists of terms like "Facebook likes" and "page views." It also doesn't help when I tell people I'm coming up with article ideas about boobs, though that was a rare occurrence for me.

It's surprisingly difficult for a lot of people, even my age, to believe that work doesn't have to consist of dress codes and gray-haired bosses. It's well-known that we live in a time where all you really need is a strong enough Wi-Fi connection to turn an idea into a business, but that doesn't mean every millennial gets to experience it.

Some of the other questions I'm asked range from the vague "How does the Internet *really* work?" to questions as personal as "Do you wear sweatpants to work every day?" For everybody's convenience, and mostly my own justification, I've put together a list answering the most common questions I've been asked since becoming that guy who works for that site that is all over your Facebook feed and Twitter. Apologies in advance if I disappoint.

Twenty-Four Truths about
Life on the Other Side of the Internet

1. We're not shotgunning beers and throwing back vodka shots throughout the workday. We usually wait to do those things until the exact moment 5 p.m. hits.

2. There are sometimes extremely cute dogs that prance around the office evoking sporadic "awws" throughout the day.

3. Imagine sitting on a couch with your closest friends talking about all the things you'd normally talk about (dating, movies, sex, hangovers, corrupt politics). This, for the most part, is how we come up with story ideas and topics to cover.

4. Nerf-gun battles have broken out during work hours. Warning: Nerf darts sting a lot more now than they did when we were children. Maybe because we're all a bit flabbier and susceptible to pain.

5. I have never worn sweatpants to work.

6. I do get to meet and talk to celebrities, but just because I meet them doesn't mean we're friends. Believe me, I've tried.

7. Running a website is not all lounging on couches and overanalyzing trends and world issues. There are meetings with agencies, advertisers, investors, and advisors. Corporate America is always close by.

8. We do have happy hour every Friday. If you can get in touch with me and guess the password I'll invite you.

9. As much as we want to say we don't read the comments on articles, we sometimes can't help it. The funniest one I've ever received was, "Your Western efforts to discredit my country will not succeed."

10. People really can make a substantial living working for a website. Writers, editors, and English majors rejoice.

11. Knowing that tens of millions of people from around the world are reading the site on a monthly basis is as exciting as it is terrifying.

12. There is no such thing as a nine-to-five when working in digital publishing.

13. Most awkward celebrity encounter: a tie between the time I asked Alesso if I could pee in his tour bus midinterview and the time I made eye contact with Steve Buscemi while he peed in the urinal next to me.

14. Having a boss (the Elite Daily founder and CEO) that is a year younger than me is not as weird as it sounds. Though he does hold it against me at times.

15. It is impossible for me to read anything on the Internet anymore without viewing it as a potential story to cover; a story I'm jealous we didn't cover first; or a story that I'm happy we covered better.

16. There is not some giant turf war between competing websites. We do not seek out Buzzfeed, the Huffington Post, and Thought Catalog employees and pelt them with eggs and water balloons. Some of us are even friends.

17. Pizza Fridays. Bagel Wednesdays.

18. No, I can't post your video rant about string cheese or the photos you took of your cat in a tiny dress. But send it to me anyway, because on second thought, maybe I will.

19. I don't speak using Internet acronyms. My laughs are real guttural heaves, not phonetically pronounced LOLs. I've never spoken the letters OMG or SMH in my life, so please STFU.

20. If I see you on your phone or laptop reading an article, I am studying every single one of your habits. How long it takes you to scroll, where your eyes move, if you click into another story, if you're only reading headlines and looking at photographs. Maybe *I am* that creep on the train.

21. One week in Internet time is roughly one year. We age differently.

22. The key to setting trends on the Internet is paying painstakingly close attention to the trends in real life. Do overalls seem to be making a comeback? Do people seem to be drinking one particular type of coffee? What global issue are people arguing most about in bars? Life online can't exist without life offline.

23. Knowing your words will live digitally online does provide a level of confidence and honesty that is difficult to attain through face-to-face interaction.

24. Yes, there is a method behind the numbers we choose for lists like this one. I can't tell you what that method is.

Point being: the Internet is a funny place when you take a peek behind the curtain. People forget it's crafted and sustained by actual living, breathing, flesh-and-blood people, who are working actual hours for actual currency to live their actual lives. You probably see us every day and don't even know it, the same way I wonder how many people I walk by every day on the streets are serial killers who have yet to be caught.

This makes me think about the girl on the train. The one with the boobs that aren't big but aren't tiny either. She's a reminder for me that outside of the four walls of the office, the work I help produce on a daily basis is actually reaching people. And not just reaching them in a way that's measured by page views and all the other metrics that are as valuable as currency in the business world of websites. Reaching people in a way that can cause an actual smile, or even an LOL on a crowded train. That has to count for something in this world.

The incident with the girl on the train was enough to keep me believing in the power of evolving communication and the influence of the written word. She must have felt the electricity of that virtual connection, too. She had to have appreciated the fact that a stranger—whether myself or one of the countless people around the world who throw their voices and personal thoughts into the digital abyss—could produce something that appeared at her fingertips and made her feel something.

But let's be real. She's probably still freaked the fuck out.

At least we got the page view.

The Art of Living
Other People's Lives

I have perfected a technique that I call wireless wiretapping. If it were a sport it would be called competitive social listening. If it were a profession, my title would be eavesdropping specialist. If it were a diagnosable condition, doctors would name it hyper-attentiveness disorder. If you're calling it like it is, the word would be *creepy*.

Over the years, I've found that the key to successful eavesdropping is simple: wear headphones but don't listen to music. Throw in a book you're not actually reading or type out a long text message you'll never send and you're all set. That way you can lean nearer to a person on a crowded train or walk unsettlingly close to a couple on the sidewalk, all while evading suspicion. People assume you're just preoccupied and not paying attention, which, lucky for me, most people in New York City are to begin with.

It's not so much a person's conversation in its entirety that interests me. It's more so the fragmented dialogue and morsels of stories we tend to catch in passing. It could be the couple arguing on the street corner or the guy that runs into someone he knows in Starbucks. How often do you walk by friends engaged in conversation and hold doors for people on the phone and suddenly, without asking for it, you've become intermingled with their words? For that brief moment, their world becomes yours.

It's like when a car playing loud music drives by and you catch a lyric or two without context. But the context doesn't matter. The words live on their own. These abrupt glimpses into the lives of others are always filling up the spaces around us, invisible but real, and it wasn't until my sophomore year in college that I began to take notice.

I was at a bus stop in Jamaica, Queens, when a couple in the middle of a conversation strolled by. But the only fragment I caught was as follows:

MAN. I swear I thought Spike Lee was Asian.

WOMAN. That's *stereotypical.*

MAN. How's that stereotypical? Asians always have the last name Lee.

For some reason the words sent a wave of excitement through my body. To me it was the perfect exchange. Hilarious yet strangely telling. It had the framework of a staged comedy bit, though the man was truly oblivious to the fact he was indeed being stereotypical. I quickly typed the words into my phone. I wasn't sure why, but I knew they needed to be saved and revisited. I decided I'd be their guardian.

The same day, back on my college campus, I walked past two girls on the way to class. When they came within earshot I overheard one say to the other, "I definitely woke up with clothes on when I know I went to bed naked."

The words echoed in my ears as if they were spoken directly to me, but as the girls made their way down the hallway, the rest of the conversation faded into inaudible static. Why the fuck did she wake up with clothes on if she went to bed naked? Was there a guy involved? Did she spend the night with the ultimate gentleman? The perfect guy that doesn't have sex on the first date and dresses the girl when she accidentally falls asleep naked? Or was he trying to cover up something more sinister? I wrote the sentence down in my phone right below the Spike Lee exchange from earlier and spent my entire class staring at them. It felt both illegal and enlightening.

Since that day I've made it a point to not only write down the strange, profound, ominous, comical, prophetic, joyful, philosophical, and straight-up insane things I hear in passing, but also to make sure I seek them out. It sounds creepy, and I suppose it is, in a way. A lot of people say, "I think I'll go for a quick walk to clear my mind and enjoy the day," but not as many people say, "I think I'll take a walk while deceptively pretending to multitask so I can write down the words of others without their knowing." My theory is, when in doubt, call your questionable habits a social experiment or say they're in the name of art.

While walking the streets of New York City alone, the portions of conversations I've overheard have been everything from heartbreaking to hilarious. There are stories unfolding every second around us. If you listen closely enough you'll find the lives of others both strikingly similar and drastically different from your own. Personally, I can't think of a better representation of our existence. Just don't get caught without your headphones. You may have some explaining to do.

Here are some of the notable blurbs I've collected over the past six years:

"Sure, I think about going to the gym. But then I think about how I'm going to die one day."

"I just really don't get why when one person gets fired everyone else doesn't just get a raise."

"I was walking home last night and saw Courtney Love peeing on a stoop."

"Show me where Kuwait is on a map and I'll give you a blow job."

"I can't do it. I can't just wake up and go to the dentist."

"The lord is my neighbor. The lord is my pen pal. The lord is my golden retriever. I don't have a golden retriever."

"I'll be late for dinner, again."

"I swear I'm not mad. Keep asking me and I will be."

"*Fuck those tiny paper cups at doctor's offices and shit.*"

"*I'm waiting for him to say 'I love you' first.*"

"*Rest in peace to the dick I once I knew.*"

"*Good luck in life.*"

"*Got that crack, X, dope . . . you need? Got Adderall for the white people, too.*"

"*Keep swiping right, you idiot.*"

"*Job titles are like eyebrows, they can change everything.*"

"*My rent money went toward the lobster in my stomach.*"

"*I'm always cold. It could be a problem. But doctor's offices are always cold, so why go?*"

"*I feel like I'm doing a lot better than most of my friends.*"

"*I get it, we're all immigrants, but we're also fucking Americans.*"

"*I want some popcorn, yo! I'm dead-ass about to buy some!*"

"*I wouldn't be mad if ISIS attacked Whole Foods.*"

"*Definitely herpes.*"

"*Is redneck a race?*"

"*My Tinder date wants to be a Bill Clinton impersonator.*"

"*Who needs love when you have Starbucks?*"

"*I'm busy Friday. And then Saturday I'm turning the fuck up in the club.*"

"*Sometimes you just gotta be your own hero and save your own little heart. Because sometimes the people you can't imagine living without can live without you.*"

"*Carla's pregnant and doesn't know how to tell her mom. She wants me to do it.*"

"I need money so bad I can't even jerk off."

"I can tell if a girl is blonde or brunette just by looking at her legs."

"Siri, where am I?"

"I was cheating on her ass the whole time anyway."

"If the Knicks win a championship before I die I'll donate my balls to science."

"It's not about the money. Trust me, it's not. It helps, but it's really not about the money."

"Do you still love me?"

"They accepted my application."

"I'm on a gluten-only diet, motherfucker."

"My boss caught me putting booze in my coffee again."

"Every dude in a relationship has a girl on the side as a backup plan."

"I didn't get in. It's okay, I wasn't expecting to anyway."

"I'm one of those guys who peaked in high school."

"You need to tell him you're worth more than the way he treats you. You should only ever feel like you want a person. Not like you need them."

"Go protest somewhere life doesn't matter, like Nebraska."

"All you need to do is tell a girl you're taking her on an adventure and she'll do anything."

"The sex wasn't the best. It also wasn't the worst. So basically marriage material."

"People are just hook-up whores these days."

"Kids are a lot like Post-It notes."

"Christmas is everybody's favorite holiday, even the Jews."

"Anxiety is great, it's like getting high without taking drugs."

*"When I cry you always say, 'Cheer up, you're not dead.' But you
    don't know if dead people are sad."*

Acknowledgments

This book wouldn't be possible without all the people out there whose lives are far more interesting than my own. Thank you for letting me observe and take notes.

I have to give a colossal thank you to my agent, Eve Attermann, and WME for sticking by my side. Thanks for taking a chance on a first-time author. A big thanks to Jessica Fromm for making this collection stronger and funnier than I ever imagined. And thanks for admitting you eavesdrop on people, too.

A huge thanks to the entire Elite Daily family. To David and Jonathon for building the dream and taking so many of us along for a wild ride. We disrupted an entire industry and learned a ton about ourselves along the way. I've never once been upset I had to get up and go to work in the morning.

I have to give a shout-out to Elite Daily's fearless editor in chief, Kaitlyn Cawley. Nothing is more fun than being your copilot. I also have to give a special thanks to Phil Portolano. The first halves of our lives are forever intertwined and our bond remains unbreakable. To Kyle for saying yes to the trips around the world and to Patrice for being there through the ups and downs. And to everyone else from back home, you know exactly who you are.

I would not have been able to stay sane throughout this writing process without my new support system and second family, the Bifulcos, and everyone else I've been blessed to get to know since meeting Brittany. And to Brittany. Thanks for being the most genuine and kind-hearted person I know. You inspire me everyday.

Nothing in my life would be possible without the endless support of my family—cousins, aunts, uncles, and all. I only hope to make you all proud.

Mom, Dad, Cole—you guys are my world and my best friends. You've taught me the values I will carry with me forever. You also all love food, and what's more important than food?

I wouldn't feel right if I didn't end this with a thank you to my grandparents, both here and no longer with us. This book is also dedicated to Nanny and Pop, who didn't need to fully understand everything I was after to know they supported it. And of course to Grammy, who knew more words than I will ever know. You taught me the power of storytelling.

Photo by Alec MacDonald

About the Author

Greg Dybec was born in Huntington Station, New York. He graduated from St. John's University in 2011 with a Bachelor's degree in English. He worked as writer and editor for a number of digital publications before joining Elite Daily in 2013. He lives in Astoria, Queens. Keep up with his work and writing at www.gregdybec.com and follow him on Twitter and Instagram @gregdybec and at Facebook.com/gregdybecauthor.